CONTENTS

INTRODUCTION

Changing to a plant-based diet is one of the most important decisions you can make to improve your health, boost energy levels, and also prevent chronic diseases. Science shows that eating more healthily helps you to live longer, can also help the environment and reduce the risk of getting sick.

Plant-based diets are really popular nowadays, and you might have heard about some of its advantages. In the long run, this diet can help you not only with your health but also your energy and make some changes that can completely change your life. You can easily find the basics of a plant-based diet in this book, it includes what you should eat, what to avoid, the benefits it has, and some recipes for beginners like you to start this new lifestyle.

This book is also beneficial for those people who have wondered about the plant-based diet but had absolutely no idea where to start. This plant-based diet cookbook is looking forward to helping people make changes in their life, starting with their diet. Nothing in will ever stop you once you start your weight loss journey.

If you want to start a plant-based diet but don't know exactly where to start, don't worry! This book is just for you. Here you can find everything so you can make this change easy and also enjoy it. Here you can find the answers to your questions, advice, and some techniques that you may need.

Some good news is that a plant-based diet makes your body stronger, so it can resist many types of chronic diseases. Some effects of these diseases can be limited or controlled, while others can be completely eliminated. Now it's your time to change your life!

Weight loss is based on a nutrient-dense diet, and it's all that is needed to achieve your goals. So if you have been trying to lose weight, now is the time to make that difference! Read patiently and carefully every section of this cookbook, and you'll understand what it is essential to know about this plant-based diet. You'll find it really interesting. The caloric density of plant-based unprocessed foods is lower, this means that the portions you eat can be larger and it will be a lot easier to lose the weight as you are consuming more food.

Once people start changing and moving to a plant-based diet, they have more motivation to eat healthy as they feel great and are capable of doing so many things.

This cookbook gives you the opportunity to nourish yourself in a simple, affordable, and delicious way. Start cooking with these plant-based recipes today as making this change could save your life!

With this cookbook, you will enjoy simple and delicious plant-based diet meals that you will love and eat again!

How a Plant-Based Diet Can Boost Your Health

Did you know that a Whole-Food, Plant-Based diet can significantly boost your health? Here is how.

Scientist proves that many chronic diseases can be reduced, reversed, or controlled by eating whole-foods and having a plant-based diet. Studies show that this type of diet can reduce the risk of type 2 diabetes, heart disease, certain types of cancer, and other important illnesses. Other benefits are more significant fitness results, more energy, less inflammation, and better health outcomes after deciding to make this change.

Whole-food, Plant-based diet

This diet is based on the following:

Whole food: natural foods are not very or heavily processed. It means minimally refined or unrefined ingredients

Plant-based: these are the food that comes from plants and has no anima ingredients (milk, honey, meat, eggs)

By eating natural, no processed foods that don't come from animals, you can meet your nutritional needs.

You'll love these foods!

Here are some of the most critical food categories that you'll enjoy in this diet:

Vegetables: a lot of veggies that include avocados, spinach, lettuce, peppers, peas, corn, kale, etc.

Whole grains: starches such as cereals and grains, quinoa, brown rice, whole wheat, oats, and other foods that are in their whole form.

Fruits: this includes bananas, citrus fruits, apples, grapes, berries, etc.

Legumes: includes beans of any type, also lentils, pulses, etc.

Tubers: these can be potatoes, carrots, sweet potatoes, parsnips, beets, etc.

Seeds, tofu, nuts, whole grain flour, and breads are other foods that you can enjoy! These foods should be eaten in moderation as they are more calorie-dense and can make you gain weight.

What are the benefits?

Science proves that having a plant-based diet brings different benefits; these include:

Managing weight efficiently: this diet helps to lose weight and keep it off without having to count calories; people who follow this diet tend to be leaner.

Prevents diseases: chronic diseases such as heart disease and diabetes can be prevented or even reversed with this diet.

Lighter environmental footprint: the plant-based diet helps to improve the environment as it reduces the stress in it.

Welcome to the plant-based diet lifestyle. Enjoy!

What to Eat and What to avoid

All recipes call for 100% plant foods: vegetables, fruits, whole grains, legumes, nuts and seeds, and contain no animal-derived ingredients: meat (beef, pork, fowl, fish, or seafood), eggs, honey, or dairy products cow's milk, cream, butter, cheese, or yogurt).

When you switch to a plant-based diet, all meals are center around plant-based foods.

Foods like eggs, dairy, meat, seafood, and poultry could be used as a complement to a plant-based meal, not as the main food.

A Whole-Foods, Plant-Based Shopping List:

Fruits: Citrus fruits, berries, peaches, pears, pineapple, bananas, etc.

Vegetables: Spinach, tomatoes, kale, peppers, broccoli, cauliflower, carrots, asparagus, etc.

Starchy vegetables: Sweet potatoes, potatoes, butternut squash, etc.

Whole grains: Rolled oats, quinoa, Brown rice, farro, brown rice pasta, barley, etc.

Healthy fats: Olive oil, avocados, coconut oil, unsweetened coconut, etc.

Legumes: Chickpeas, lentils, peas, peanuts, black beans, etc.

Seeds, nuts, and nut butters: Cashews, macadamia, almonds, nuts, sunflower seeds, natural peanut butter, pumpkin seeds, tahini, etc.

Unsweetened plant-based milks: almond milk, cashew milk, Coconut milk, etc.

Spices, herbs and seasonings: Rosemary, turmeric, basil, curry, black pepper, salt, etc.

Condiments: Nutritional yeast, soy sauce, salsa, mustard, vinegar, lemon juice, etc.

Plant-based protein: Tempeh, plant-based protein sources, Tofu, or powders with no added sugar or artificial ingredients.

Beverages: Sparkling water, Coffee, tea, etc.

AVOID THIS FOODS

Meat: Seafood, red meat, fish, poultry, processed meat.

Dairy: Butter, half and half, yogurt, milk, cheese, cream, buttermilk.

Eggs: Chicken, duck, quail, ostrich.

Plant Fragments (these oftentimes include Plant-based replacement foods): Margarine, Added Fats, oils*

*Oil, including olive oil, is 100% fat, nutrient-poor, and calorically-dense. Oil injures the innermost lining of the artery, the endothelium, and that injury is the gateway to vascular disease. For people with known heart disease, even adding a little oil can have a negative impact on heart health.

Refined Sugar: White sugar, beet sugar, brown rice syrup, barley malt, cane juice crystals, cane sugar, brown sugar, corn syrup, confectioner's sugar, fructose.

Refined Grains: White rice, quick-cook oats, white flour.

Protein Isolates: Pea protein isolate, Soy protein isolate, seitan.

Beverages: Fruit juice (even 100% pure fruit juice), Soda, sports drinks, energy drinks.

21-DAYS MEAL PLAN

DAY: 1

Breakfast: Fruity Granola (15)

Lunch: Pesto & White Bean Pasta (106)

Dinner: Golden Harvest Soup (45)

DAY:2

Breakfast: Pumpkin Steel-Cut Oats (15)

Lunch: Green Pea Risotto (84) And Caramelized Onion

And Beet Salad (149)

Dinner: Minty Beet and Sweet Potato Soup (46)

DAY:3

Breakfast: Chocolate Quinoa Breakfast Bowl (16)

Lunch: Grilled Portobello with Mashed Potatoes and

Green Beans (115)

Dinner: Weeknight Chickpea Tomato Soup (40)

DAY:4

Breakfast:Muesli and Berries Bowl (17)

Lunch: Italian Lentils (98)

Dinner: Tomato Orzo Soup (82)

DAY:5

Breakfast: Cinnamon And Spice Overnight Oats (18)

Lunch: Roasted Cauliflower Tacos (117)

Dinner: Creamy Avocado-Dressed Kale Salad (157)

DAY:6

Breakfast: Baked Banana French Toast with Raspberry

Syrup (19)

Lunch: White Bean Burgers (114)

Dinner: Minty Beet and Sweet Potato Soup(46)

DAY:7

Breakfast: Sunshine Muffins (20)

Lunch: Loaded Black Bean Pizza (95)

Dinner: Creamy Butternut Squash Soup (55)

DAY:8

Breakfast: Smoothie Breakfast Bowl (21)

Lunch: Spanish Rice And Beans (106)

Dinner: Tabbouleh Salad (154)

DAY:9

Breakfast: Savory Pancakes (23)

Lunch: Curried Mango Chickpea Wrap (93)

Dinner: Cream of Mushroom Soup (59)

DAY:10

Breakfast: Tropi-Kale Breeze (24)

Lunch: Lemony Lentil And Rice Soup (81)

Dinner: Glazed Curried Carrots (123)

DAY:11

Breakfast: Blueberry Oatmeal Breakfast Bars (26)

Lunch: GGB Bowl (110)

Dinner:Hot & Sour Tofu Soup (60)

DAY:12

Breakfast: Banana Bread Rice Pudding (32)

Lunch: Ratatouille (Pressure cooker) (125)

Dinner: Rainbow Quinoa Salad (161)

DAY:13

Breakfast: Orange French Toast (27)

Lunch: Lemon and Thyme Couscous (88)

Dinner: Tempeh And Vegetable Stir-Fry (139)

DAY:14

Breakfast: Oatmeal Raisin Breakfast Cookie (27)

Lunch: Sushi-Style Quinoa (128)

Dinner: Eggplant Parmesan (144)

DAY:15

Breakfast: Chocolate Quinoa Breakfast Bowl (16)

Lunch: Lentil Spinach Curry (113)

Dinner: Apple-Sunflower Spinach Salad (165)

DAY:16

Breakfast: Quinoa Applesauce Muffins (28)

Lunch:Vegetable and Barley Stew (Pressure Cooker) (52)

Dinner: Moroccan Aubergine Salad (51)

DAY:17

Breakfast: Pumpkin Pancakes (29)

Lunch: Mindful Mushroom Stroganoff (142)

Dinner: Spaghetti Squash Primavera (141)

DAY:18

Breakfast: Warm Quinoa Breakfast Bowl (32)

Lunch: Balsamic Black Beans (103)

Dinner: Red Peppers and Kale (144)

DAY:19

Breakfast: Maple-Pecan Waffles (23)

Lunch: Brown Rice and Lentils (91)

Dinner: Not-Tuna Salad (152)

DAY:20

Breakfast: Breakfast Parfaits (34)

Lunch: Maple Dijon Burgers(127)

Dinner: Caesar Salad(174)

DAY:21

Breakfast: Spiced Orange Breakfast Couscous (33)

Lunch: Maple-Bourbon Acorn Squash (140)

Dinner: Warm Vegetable "Salad" (148)

BREAKFAST

Orange French Toast

Prep: 15 Minutes • Cook Time: 10 Minutes • Total: 25 Minutes• Serves: 4

Ingredients

3 very ripe bananas

1 cup unsweetened nondairy milk

zest and juice of 1 orange

1 teaspoon ground cinnamon

¼ teaspoon grated nutmeg

4 slices french bread

1 tablespoon coconut oil

Directions

1.   Preparing the Ingredients.

In a blender, combine the bananas, almond milk, orange juice and zest, cinnamon, and nutmeg, then blend until smooth. Pour the mixture into a 9-by-13-inch baking dish. Soak the bread in the mixture for 5 minutes on each side.

2.   Cook

While the bread soaks, heat a griddle or sauté pan over medium-high heat. Melt the coconut oil in the pan and swirl to coat. Cook the bread slices until golden brown on both sides for about 5 minutes each. Serve immediately.

Oatmeal Raisin Breakfast Cookie

Prep: 5 Minutes • Cook Time: 15 Minutes • Total:20 Minutes• Serves: 2 Cookies

Ingredients

½ cup rolled oats

1 tablespoon whole-wheat flour

½ teaspoon baking powder

1 to 2 tablespoons brown sugar

½ teaspoon pumpkin pie spice or ground cinnamon (optional)

¼ cup unsweetened applesauce, plus more as needed

2 tablespoons raisins, dried cranberries, or vegan chocolate chips

Directions

1.   Preparing the Ingredients.

In a medium bowl, stir together the oats, flour, baking powder, sugar, and pumpkin pie spice (if using). Stir in the applesauce until thoroughly combined. Add another

1 to 2 tablespoons of applesauce if the mixture looks too dry (this will depend on the type of oats used).

Shape the mixture into 2 cookies.

2. Bake

Put them on a microwave-safe plate and heat them on high power for 90 seconds. Alternatively, bake on a small tray in a 350°F oven or toaster oven for 15 minutes. Let it cool slightly before eating.

Per Serving (2 cookies): Calories: 175; Protein: 74g; Total fat: 2g; Saturated fat:0g; Carbohydrates: 39g; Fiber: 4g

Blueberry Oat Muffins

Prep: 10 Minutes • Cook Time: 20 Minutes • Total:30 Minutes• Serves: 12 Muffins

Ingredients

2 tablespoons coconut oil or vegan margarine, melted, plus more for preparing the muffin tin

1 cup quick-cooking oats or instant oats

1 cup boiling water

½ cup nondairy milk

¼ cup ground flaxseed

1 teaspoon vanilla extract

1 teaspoon apple cider vinegar

1½ cups whole-wheat flour

½ cup brown sugar

2 teaspoons baking soda

Pinch salt

1 cup blueberries

Directions

1. Preparing the Ingredients.

Preheat the oven to 400°F.

Coat a muffin tin with coconut oil, line with paper muffin cups, or use a nonstick tin.

In a large bowl, combine the oats and boiling water. Stir so the oats soften. Add the coconut oil, milk, flaxseed, vanilla, and vinegar and stir to combine. Add the flour, sugar, baking soda, and salt. Stir until combined. Gently fold in the blueberries. Scoop the muffin mixture into the prepared tin, about ⅓ cup for each muffin.

2. Bake

Bake for 20 to 25 minutes until slightly browned on top and springy to the touch. Let it cool for about 10 minutes. Run a dinner knife around the inside of each cup to loosen, then tilt the muffins on their sides in the muffin wells so air gets underneath. These keep in an airtight container in the refrigerator for up to 1 week or in the freezer indefinitely.

Per Serving (1muffin): Calories: 174; Protein: 5g; Total fat: 3g; Saturated fat:2g; Carbohydrates: 33g; Fiber: 4g

Quinoa Applesauce Muffins

Prep: 10 Minutes • Cook Time: 15 Minutes • Total:25 Minutes• Serves: 5

Ingredients

2 tablespoons coconut oil or vegan margarine, melted, plus more for coating the muffin tin

¼ cup ground flaxseed

½ cup water

2 cups unsweetened applesauce

½ cup brown sugar

1 teaspoon apple cider vinegar

2½ cups whole-wheat flour

1½ cups cooked quinoa

2 teaspoons baking soda

Pinch salt

½ cup dried cranberries or raisins

Directions

1. **Preparing the Ingredients.**

Preheat the oven to 400°F.

Coat a muffin tin with coconut oil, line with paper muffin cups, or use a nonstick tin. In a large bowl, stir together the flaxseed and water. Add the applesauce, sugar, coconut oil, and vinegar. Stir to combine. Add the flour, quinoa, baking soda, and salt, stirring until just combined. Gently fold in the cranberries without stirring too much. Scoop the muffin mixture into the prepared tin, about ⅓ cup for each muffin.

2. **Bake**

Bake for 15 to 20 minutes, until slightly browned on top and springy to the touch. Let cool for about 10 minutes. Run a dinner knife around the inside of each cup to loosen, then tilt the muffins on their sides in the muffin wells so air gets underneath. These keep in an airtight container in the refrigerator for up to 1 week or in the freezer indefinitely.

Per Serving(1muffin): Calories: 387; Protein: 7g; Total fat: 5g; Saturated fat: 2g; Carbohydrates: 57g; Fiber: 8g

Pumpkin Pancakes

Prep: 15 Minutes • Cook Time: 15 Minutes • Total:30 Minutes• Serves: 4

Ingredients

2 cups unsweetened almond milk

1 teaspoon apple cider vinegar

2½ cups whole-wheat flour

2 tablespoons baking powder

½ teaspoon baking soda

1 teaspoon sea salt

1 teaspoon pumpkin pie spice or

½ teaspoon ground -cinnamon plus

¼ teaspoon grated -nutmeg plus

¼ teaspoon ground allspice

½ cup canned pumpkin purée

1 cup water

1 tablespoon coconut oil

Directions

1. **Preparing the Ingredients.**

In a small bowl, combine the almond milk and apple cider vinegar. Set aside.

In a large bowl, whisk together the flour, baking powder, baking soda, salt, and pumpkin pie spice. In another large bowl, combine the almond milk mixture, pumpkin purée, and water, whisking to mix well. Add the wet ingredients to the dry ingredients and fold together until the dry ingredients are moistened.

2. **Bake**

In a nonstick pan or griddle over medium-high heat, melt the coconut oil and swirl to coat. Pour the batter into the pan ¼ cup at a time, and cook until the pancakes are browned, about 5 minutes per side. Serve immediately

Green Breakfast Smoothie

Prep: 10 Minutes • Cook Time: 0 Minutes • Total: 10 Minutes • Serves: 2

Ingredients

½ banana, sliced

2 Cups Spinach or other greens, such as kale

1 Cup sliced berries of your choosing, fresh or frozen

1 orange, peeled and cut into segments

1 cup unsweetened nondairy milk

1 cup ice

Directions

1. **Preparing the Ingredients**

In a blender, combine all the ingredients.

Starting with the blender on low speed, begin blending the smoothie, gradually increasing blender speed until smooth. Serve immediately.

Blueberry Lemonade Smoothie

Prep: 5 Minutes • Cook Time: 0 Minutes • Total: 5 Minutes • Serves: 1

Ingredients

1 cup roughly chopped kale

¾ cup frozen blueberries

1 cup unsweetened soy or almond milk

Juice of 1 lemon

1 tablespoon maple syrup

Directions

1. **Preparing the Ingredients**

Combine all the ingredients in a blender and blend until smooth. Enjoy immediately.

Berry Protein Smoothie

Prep: 5 Minutes • Cook Time: 0 Minutes • Total:5 Minutes • Serves: 1

Ingredients

1 banana

1 cup fresh or frozen berries

¾ cup water or nondairy milk, plus more as needed

1 scoop plant-based protein powder, 3 ounces silken tofu, ¼ cup rolled oats, or ½ cup cooked quinoa

Additions

1 tablespoon ground flaxseed or chia seeds

1 handful fresh spinach or lettuce, or 1 chunk cucumber

coconut water to replace some of the liquid

Directions

1. **Preparing the Ingredients**

In a blender, combine the banana, berries, water, and your choice of protein.

Add any addition ingredients as desired. Purée until smooth and creamy for about 50 seconds.

Add a bit more water if you like a thinner smoothie

Per Serving: Calories: 332; Protein: 7g; Total fat: 5g; Saturated fat: 1g; Carbohydrates: 72g; Fiber: 11g

Berry Beetsicle Smoothie

Prep: 3 Minutes • Cook Time: 0Minutes • Total:3 Minutes• Serves: 1

Ingredients

½ cup peeled and diced beets

½ cup frozen raspberries

1 frozen banana

1 tablespoon pure maple syrup

1 cup unsweetened soy or almond milk

Directions

1. **Preparing the Ingredients.**

Combine all the ingredients in a blender and blend until smooth.

Blueberry and Chia Smoothie

Prep: 10 Minutes • Cook Time: 0 Minutes • Total: 10 Minutes • Serves: 2

Ingredients

2 tablespoons chia seeds

2 cups unsweetened nondairy milk

2 cups blueberries, fresh or frozen

2 tablespoons pure maple syrup or agave

2 tablespoons cocoa powder

Directions

1. **Preparing the Ingredients**

Soak the chia seeds in the almond milk for 5 minutes.

In a blender, combine the soaked chia seeds, almond milk, blueberries, maple syrup, and cocoa powder and blend until smooth. Serve immediately.

Green Kickstart Smoothie

Prep: 5 Minutes • Cook Time: 0 Minutes • Total: 5 Minutes • Serves: 1

Ingredients

½ avocado or 1 banana

½ cup chopped cucumber, peeled if desired

1 handful fresh spinach or chopped lettuce

1 pear or apple, peeled and cored, or 1 cup unsweetened applesauce

2 tablespoons freshly squeezed lime juice

1 cup water or nondairy milk, plus more as needed

Additions

½-inch piece peeled fresh ginger

1 tablespoon ground flaxseed or chia seeds

½ cup soy yogurt or 3 ounces silken tofu

coconut water to replace some of the liquid

2 tablespoons chopped fresh mint or

½ cup chopped mango

Directions

1. **Preparing the Ingredients**

In a blender, combine the avocado, cucumber, spinach, pear, lime juice, and water.

Add any additional ingredients as desired. Purée until smooth and creamy, about 50 seconds. Add a bit more water if you like a thinner smoothie.

Per Serving: Calories: 263; Protein: 4g; Total fat: 14g; Saturated fat: 2g; Carbohydrates: 36g; Fiber: 10g

Warm Maple and Cinnamon Quinoa

Prep: 5 Minutes • Cook Time: 15 Minutes • Total: 20 Minutes • Serves: 4

Ingredients

1 cup unsweetened nondairy milk

1 cup water

1 cup quinoa, rinsed

1 teaspoon cinnamon

¼ cup chopped pecans or other nuts or seeds, such as chia, sunflower seeds, or almonds

2 tablespoons pure maple syrup or agave

Directions

1. **Preparing the Ingredients**

In a medium saucepan over medium-high heat, bring the almond milk, water, and quinoa to a boil. Lower the heat to medium-low and cover. Simmer until the liquid is mostly absorbed and the quinoa softens, for about 15 minutes.

2. **Finish and serve**

Turn off the heat and allow to sit, covered, for 5 minutes. Stir in the cinnamon, pecans, and syrup. Serve hot.

Warm Quinoa Breakfast Bowl

Prep: 5 Minutes • Cook Time: 0 Minutes • Total: 5 Minutes • Serves: 4

Ingredients

3 cups freshly cooked quinoa

1⅓ cups unsweetened soy or almond milk

2 bananas, sliced

1 cup raspberries

1 cup blueberries

½ cup chopped raw walnuts

Directions

1. **Preparing the Ingredients**

Divide the ingredients among 4 bowls, starting with a base of ¾ cup quinoa, ⅓ cup milk, ½ banana, ¼ cup raspberries, ¼ cup blueberries, and 2 tablespoons walnuts.

Banana Bread Rice Pudding

Prep: 5 Minutes • Cook Time: 50 Minutes • Total: 55 Minutes • Serves: 4

Ingredients

1cup brown rice

1½ cups water

1½ cups nondairy milk

3 tablespoons sugar (omit if using a sweetened nondairy milk)

2 teaspoons pumpkin pie spice or ground cinnamon

2 bananas

3 tablespoons chopped walnuts or sunflower seeds (optional)

Directions

1. **Preparing the Ingredients**

In a medium pot, combine the rice, water, milk, sugar, and pumpkin pie spice. Bring to a boil over high heat, turn the heat to low, and cover the pot. Simmer, stirring occasionally, until the rice is soft and the liquid is absorbed. White rice takes about 20 minutes; while brown rice takes about 50 minutes to cook.

Smash the bananas and stir them into the cooked rice.

2. **Finish and Serve**

Serve topped with walnuts (if using). Leftovers will keep refrigerated in an airtight container for up to 5 days.

Per Serving: Calories: 479; Protein: 9g; Total fat: 13g; Saturated fat: 1g; Carbohydrates: 86g; Fiber: 7g

Apple and Cinnamon Oatmeal

Prep: 10 Minutes • Cook Time:10 Minutes • Total: 20 Minutes • Serves: 2

Ingredients

1¼ cups apple cider

1 apple, peeled, cored, and chopped

⅔ cup rolled oats

1 teaspoon ground cinnamon

1 tablespoon pure maple syrup or agave
(optional)

Directions

1. Preparing the Ingredients.

In a medium saucepan, bring the apple cider to a boil over medium-high heat. Stir in the apple, oats, and cinnamon.

Bring the cereal to a boil and turn down heat to low. Simmer until the oatmeal thickens for 3 to 4 minutes.

2. Finish and serve

Spoon into two bowls and sweeten with maple syrup, if using. Serve hot.

Breakfast Parfaits

Prep: 15 Minutes • Cook Time: 0 Minutes • Total: 15 Minutes • Serves: 2

Ingredients

one 14-ounce can coconut milk, refrigerated overnight

1 cup granola

½ cup walnuts

1 cup sliced strawberries or other seasonal berries

Directions

1.   Preparing the Ingredients.

Pour off the canned coconut-milk liquid and retain the solids.

2.   Finish and Serve

In two parfait glasses, layer the coconut-milk solids, granola, walnuts, and -strawberries. Serve immediately.

Sweet Potato and Kale Hash

Prep: 10 Minutes • Cook Time: 15 Minutes • Total: 25 Minutes • Serves: 2

Ingredients

1 sweet potato

2 tablespoons extra-virgin olive oil

½ onion, chopped

1 carrot, peeled and chopped

2 garlic cloves, minced

½ teaspoon dried thyme

1 cup chopped kale

sea salt

freshly ground black pepper

Directions

1. Preparing the Ingredients.

Prick the sweet potato with a fork and microwave on high until soft, for about 5 minutes. Remove from the microwave and cut into ¼-inch cubes.

2. Cook

In a large nonstick sauté pan, heat the olive oil over medium-high heat. Add the onion and carrot and cook until softened, for about 5 minutes. Add the garlic and thyme and cook until the garlic is fragrant, for about 30 seconds.

Add the sweet potatoes and cook until the potatoes begin to brown, about 7 -minutes. Add the kale and cook just until it wilts for 1 to 2 minutes.

3. Finish and Serve

Season with salt and pepper. Serve immediately.

SOUPS AND STEWS

Creamy Potato-Cauliflower Soup

Prep: 10 Minutes • Cook Time: 25 Minutes • Total: 35 Minutes • Serves: 6

Ingredients

1 teaspoon extra-virgin olive oil

1 onion, chopped

3 cups chopped cauliflower

2 potatoes, scrubbed or peeled and chopped

6 cups water or Vegetable Broth

2 tablespoons dried herbs

Salt

Freshly ground black pepper

1 or 2 scallions, white and light green parts only, sliced

Directions

1.   Preparing the Ingredients

Heat the olive oil in a large soup pot over medium-high heat.

Add the onion and cauliflower, and sauté for about 5 minutes, until the vegetables are slightly softened. Add the potatoes, water, and dried herbs, and season to taste with salt and pepper. Bring the soup to a boil, reduce the heat to low, and cover the pot. Simmer for 15 to 20 minutes, until the potatoes are soft.

2.   Finish and Serve

Using a hand blender, purée the soup until smooth. (Alternatively, let it cool slightly, then transfer to a countertop blender.) Stir in the scallions and serve. Leftovers will keep in an airtight container for up to 1 week in the refrigerator or up to 1 month in the freezer.

Per Serving (2 cups) Calories: 80; Protein: 2g; Total fat: 1g; Saturated fat: 0g; Carbohydrates: 17g; Fiber: 3g

Spicy Pinto Bean Soup

Prep: 5 Minutes • Cook Time: 25 Minutes • Total: 30 Minutes • Serves: 4 Servings

Ingredients

4½ cups cooked or 3 (15.5-ounce) cans pinto beans, drained and rinsed

1 (14.5-ounce) can crushed tomatoes

1 teaspoon chipotle chile in adobo

2 tablespoons extra-virgin olive oil

1 medium onion, chopped

¼cup chopped celery

2 garlic cloves, minced

½ teaspoon ground cumin

½ teaspoon dried oregano

4 cups vegetable broth, homemade or water

Salt and freshly ground black pepper

2 tablespoons chopped fresh cilantro, for garnish

Directions

1. **Preparing the Ingredients**

In a food processor, purée 1 ½ cups of the pinto beans with the tomatoes and chipotle. Set aside.

In a large soup pot, heat the oil over medium heat. Add the onion, celery, and garlic. Cover and cook until soft, stirring occasionally for about 10 minutes. Stir in the cumin, oregano, broth, puréed bean mixture, and the remaining 3 cups of beans. Season with salt and pepper. Bring to boil and reduce the heat to low and simmer, uncovered, stirring occasionally until the flavors are incorporated and the soup is hot, for about 15 minutes.

2. **Finish and Serve**

Ladle into bowls, garnish with cilantro, then serve.

Black And Gold Gazpacho

Prep: 15 Minutes • Cook Time: 0 Minutes • Total: 15 Minutes • Serves: 4 Servings

Ingredients

1½ pounds ripe yellow tomatoes, chopped

1 large cucumber, peeled, seeded, and chopped

1 large yellow bell pepper, seeded, and chopped

4 green onions, white part only

2 garlic cloves, minced

2 tablespoons extra-virgin olive oil

2 tablespoons white wine vinegar

Salt

Ground cayenne

1½ cups cooked or 1 (15.5-ounce) can black beans, drained and rinsed

2 tablespoons minced fresh parsley

1 cup toasted croutons (optional)

Directions

1. **Preparing the Ingredients**

In a blender or food processor, combine half the tomatoes with cucumber, bell pepper, green onions, and garlic. Process until smooth. Add the oil and vinegar, season with salt and cayenne, then process until blended.

2. **Finish and Serve**

Transfer the soup to a large nonmetallic bowl and stir in the black beans and remaining tomatoes. Cover the bowl and refrigerate for 1 to 2 hours. Taste and adjust seasonings if necessary.

Ladle the soup into bowls, garnish with parsley and croutons if using, then serve.

Black-Eyed Pea & Sweet Potato Soup

Prep: 10 Minutes • Cook Time: 25 Minutes • Total: 35 Minutes • Serves: 4

Ingredients

1 teaspoon extra-virgin olive oil

2 to 3 cups peeled, cubed sweet potato, squash, or pumpkin

½ onion, chopped

1 garlic clove, minced

Salt

2 cups water

1 (15-ounce) can black-eyed peas, drained and rinsed

2 tablespoons freshly squeezed lime juice

1 tablespoon sugar

1 teaspoon smoked or regular paprika

Pinch red pepper flakes or cayenne pepper

3 cups shredded cabbage

1 cup corn kernels, thawed if frozen, drained if canned

Directions

1. Preparing the Ingredients

Heat the olive oil in a large soup pot over medium-high heat.

Add the sweet potato, onion, garlic, and a pinch of salt. Sauté for 3 to 4 minutes until the onion and garlic are softened. Add the water, black-eyed peas, lime juice, sugar, paprika, red pepper flakes, and salt. Bring to a boil and cook for 15 minutes. Add the cabbage and corn to the pot, stir to combine, then cook for 5 minutes more, or until the sweet potato is tender.

2. Finish and Serve

Turn off the heat, let cool for a few minutes, and serve. Leftovers will keep in an airtight container for up to 1 week in the refrigerator, or up to 1 month in the freezer.

Per Serving (2 cups) Calories: 224; Protein: 9g; Total fat: 2g; Saturated fat: 0g; Carbohydrates: 46g; Fiber: 10g

Soba And Green Lentil Soup

Prep: 5 Minutes • Cook Time: 55 Minutes • Total: 60 Minutes • Serves: 4 To 6 Servings

Ingredients

2 tablespoons extra-virgin olive oil

1 medium onion, minced

1 medium carrot, halved lengthwise and sliced diagonally

2 garlic cloves, minced

1 (28-ounce) can crushed tomatoes

1 cup green (French) lentils, picked over, rinsed, and drained

1 teaspoon dried thyme

6 cups vegetable broth, homemade or store-bought, or water

Salt and freshly ground black pepper

4 ounces soba noodles, broken into thirds

Directions

1. Preparing the Ingredients

In a large soup pot over medium heat, heat the oil. Add the onion, carrot, and garlic. Cover and cook until softened for about 7 minutes. Uncover and stir in the tomatoes, lentils, thyme, and broth, then bring to boil. Reduce heat to medium, season with salt and pepper, then cover and simmer until the lentils are tender. Cook for about 45 minutes.

2.   Finish and Serve

Stir in the noodles and cook until tender for about 10 minutes longer, then serve.

Black Bean Soup

Prep: 10 Minutes • Cook Time: 15 Minutes • Total: 25 Minutes • Serves: 4

Ingredients

2 tablespoons extra-virgin olive oil

1 onion, diced

1 green bell pepper, diced

1 carrot, peeled and diced

4 garlic cloves, minced

two 15-ounce cans black beans, drained and rinsed

2 cups vegetable stock

¼ teaspoon ground cumin

1 teaspoon sea salt

¼ cup chopped cilantro, for garnish

Directions

1.   Preparing the Ingredients.

In a large soup pot, heat the olive oil over medium-high heat until it shimmers.

Add the onion, bell pepper, and carrot and cook until the vegetables soften for about 5 minutes. Add garlic and cook until it is fragrant. Add the black beans, vegetable stock, cumin, and salt. Cook over medium-high heat, stirring occasionally for about 10 minutes.

2.   Finish and Serve

Remove from the heat. Using a potato masher, mash the beans lightly and leave some chunks in the soup. For a smoother soup, process in a blender or food processor. Serve hot, garnished with cilantro.

Creamy Garlic-Spinach Rotini Soup

Prep: 10 Minutes • Cook Time: 15 Minutes • Total: 25 Minutes • Serves: 4

Ingredients

1 teaspoon extra-virgin olive oil

1 cup chopped mushrooms

¼ teaspoon plus a pinch salt

4 garlic cloves, minced, or 1 teaspoon garlic powder

2 peeled carrots or ½ red bell pepper, chopped

6 cups Vegetable Broth or water

Pinch freshly ground black pepper

1 cup rotini or gnocchi

¾ cup unsweetened nondairy milk

¼ cup nutritional yeast

2 cups chopped fresh spinach

¼ cup pitted black olives or sun-dried tomatoes, chopped

Herbed Croutons, for topping (optional)

Directions

1. Preparing the Ingredients

Heat the olive oil in a large soup pot over medium-high heat.

Add the mushrooms and a pinch of salt. Sauté for about 4 minutes until the mushrooms soften. Add the garlic (if using fresh) and carrots, then sauté for 1 minute. Add the vegetable broth, then add the remaining ¼ teaspoon of salt, and pepper (plus the garlic powder if using). Bring to boil and add the pasta. Cook for about 10 minutes until the pasta is cooked.

2. Finish and Serve

Turn off the heat and stir in the milk, nutritional yeast, spinach, and olives. Top with croutons (if using). Leftovers will keep in an airtight container for up to 1 week in the refrigerator, or up to 1 month in the freezer.

Per Serving (2 cups) Calories: 207; Protein: 11g; Total fat: 5g; Saturated fat: 1g; Carbohydrates: 34g; Fiber: 7g

Roasted Vegetable Bisque

Prep: 10 Minutes • Cook Time: 15 Minutes • Total: 25 Minutes • Serves: 6 Servings

Ingredients

1 large onion, coarsely chopped

2 medium carrots, coarsely chopped

1 large russet potato, peeled and cut into ½-inch dice

1 medium zucchini, thinly sliced

1 large ripe tomato, quartered

2 garlic cloves, crushed

2 tablespoons extra-virgin olive oil

½ teaspoon dried savory

½ teaspoon dried thyme

Salt and freshly ground black pepper

4 cups vegetable broth, homemade or store-bought, or water

1 tablespoon minced fresh parsley, for garnish

Directions

1. Preparing the Ingredients

Preheat the oven to 400°F. In a lightly oiled 9 x 13-inch baking pan, place the onion, carrots, potato, zucchini, tomato, and garlic. Drizzle with the oil and season with savory, thyme, and salt, and pepper to taste.

2. Bake

Cover tightly with foil and bake until softened for about 30 minutes. Uncover and bake, stirring once until the vegetables are lightly browned.

3. Finish and Serve

Transfer the roasted vegetables to a large soup pot, add the broth, and bring to boil. Reduce the heat to low and simmer, uncovered, for 15 minutes.

Purée the soup in the pot with an immersion blender or food processor, in batches if necessary, then return to the pot. Heat over medium heat until hot. Taste, adjusting seasonings if necessary.

Ladle into bowls, sprinkle with parsley, then serve

Spicy Gazpacho

Prep: 15 Minutes • Cook Time: 0 Minutes • Total: 15 Minutes • Serves: 4

Ingredients

1 tablespoon extra-virgin olive oil

3 cups vegetable juice

1 red onion, diced

3 tomatoes, chopped

1 red bell pepper, diced

2 garlic cloves, minced

juice of 1 lemon

2 tablespoons chopped fresh basil

¼ to ½ teaspoon cayenne pepper

sea salt

freshly ground black pepper

Directions

1.   Preparing the Ingredients.

In a blender or food processor, combine the olive oil, vegetable juice, all but ½ cup of the onion, all but ½ cup of the tomato, all but ½ cup of the bell pepper, the garlic, lemon juice, basil, and cayenne. Season with salt and pepper, then process until smooth.

2.   Finish and Serve

Stir the reserved ½ cup onion, ½ cup tomatoes, and ½ cup bell pepper into the processed ingredients and refrigerate for 1 hour. Serve chilled.

Mushroom & Wild Rice Stew

Prep: 10 Minutes • Cook Time: 50 Minutes • Total: 60 Minutes • Serves: 6

Ingredients

1 to 2 teaspoons extra-virgin olive oil

2 cups chopped mushrooms

½ to 1 teaspoon salt

1 onion, chopped, or 1 teaspoon onion powder

3 or 4 garlic cloves, minced, or ½ teaspoon garlic powder

1 tablespoon dried herbs

¾ cup brown rice

¼ cup wild rice or additional brown rice

3 cups water

3 cups Vegetable Broth or store-bought broth

2 to 4 tablespoons balsamic vinegar (optional)

Freshly ground black pepper

1 cup frozen peas, thawed

1 cup unsweetened nondairy milk (optional)

1 to 2 cups chopped greens, such as spinach, kale, or chard

Directions

1. **Preparing the Ingredients**

Heat the olive oil in a large soup pot over medium-high heat.

Add the mushrooms and a pinch of salt, and sauté for about 4 minutes, until the mushrooms are softened. Add the onion and garlic (if using fresh), and sauté for 1 to 2 minutes more. Stir in the dried herbs (plus the onion powder and/or garlic powder, if using), white or brown rice, wild rice, water, vegetable broth, vinegar (if using), and salt and pepper to taste. Bring to a boil, turn the heat to low, and cover the pot. Simmer the soup for 15 minutes (for white rice) or 45 minutes (for brown rice).

2. **Finish and Serve**

Turn off the heat and stir in the peas, milk (if using), and greens. Let the greens wilt before serving.

Leftovers will keep in an airtight container for up to 1 week in the refrigerator or up to 1 month in the freezer.

Per Serving (2 cups) Calories: 201; Protein: 6g; Total fat: 3g; Saturated fat: 0g; Carbohydrates: 44g; Fiber: 4g

Almond Soup With Cardamom

Prep: 5 Minutes • Cook Time: 35 Minutes • Total: 40Minutes • Serves: 4 Servings

Ingredients

1 tablespoon extra-virgin olive oil

1 medium onion, chopped

1 medium russet potato, chopped

1 medium red bell pepper, chopped

4 cups vegetable broth, homemade or water

½ teaspoon ground cardamom

Salt and freshly ground black pepper

½ cup almond butter

¼ cup sliced toasted almonds, for garnish

Directions

1. **Preparing the Ingredients**

In a large soup pot, heat the oil over medium heat. Add the onion, potato, and bell pepper. Cover and cook until softened for about 5 minutes. Add the broth, cardamom, and salt and pepper to taste. Bring to a boil, then reduce heat to low and simmer, uncovered, until the vegetables are tender for about 30 minutes.

Add the almond butter and purée in the pot with an immersion blender or food processor, in batches if necessary, then return to the pot.

2. **Finish and Serve**

Reheat over medium heat until hot. Taste and adjust seasonings if necessary, then add more broth or soy milk if needed for desired consistency.

Ladle the soup into bowls, sprinkle with toasted sliced almonds, then serve.

Easy Corn Chowder

Prep: 15 Minutes • Cook Time: 15 Minutes • Total: 30 Minutes • Serves: 4

Ingredients

2 tablespoons olive oil or other vegetable oil, such as coconut oil

1 onion, chopped

1 cup chopped fennel bulb or celery

2 carrots, peeled and chopped

1 red bell pepper, finely chopped

¼ cup all-purpose flour

6 cups vegetable stock

2 cups fresh or canned corn

2 cups cubed red potato

1 cup unsweetened almond milk or other unsweetened nut or grain milk

½ teaspoon sriracha sauce or chili paste (optional)

sea salt

freshly ground black pepper

Directions

1. **Preparing the Ingredients**

In a large pot, heat the olive oil over medium-high heat until it shimmers.

Add the onion, fennel, carrots, and bell pepper and cook, stirring occasionally, until the vegetables soften, about 3 minutes.

Sprinkle the flour over the vegetables and continue to cook, stirring constantly, for about 2 minutes.

Stir in the vegetable stock, using a spoon to scrape any bits of flour or vegetables from the bottom ofthe pan. Continue stirring until the liquid comes to a boil and the soup begins to thicken. Lower the heat to medium.

2. **Finish and Serve**

Add the corn, potatoes, almond milk, and Sriracha, if using. Simmer until the potatoes are soft, about 10 minutes. Season with salt and pepper. Serve hot.

Tamarind Chickpea Stew

Prep: 5 Minutes • Cook Time: 60 Minutes • Total: 65 Minutes • Serves: 4 Servings

Ingredients

1 tablespoon extra-virgin olive oil

1 large onion, chopped

2 medium Yukon Gold potatoes, peeled and cut into 1/4-inch dice

3 cups cooked chickpeas or 2 (15.5-ounce) cans chickpeas, drained and rinsed

1 (28-ounce) can crushed tomatoes

1 (4-ounce) can mild chopped green chiles, drained

2 tablespoons tamarind paste

¼ cup pure maple syrup

1 cup vegetable broth, homemade or water

2 tablespoons chili powder

1 teaspoon ground coriander

½ teaspoon ground cumin

Salt and freshly ground black pepper

1 cup frozen baby peas, thawed

Directions

1. **Preparing the Ingredients**

In a large saucepan, heat the oil over medium heat. Add the onion, cover, and cook until softened for about 5 minutes. Add the potatoes, chickpeas, tomatoes, and chiles, then simmer, uncovered for about 5 minutes.

In a small bowl, combine the tamarind paste, maple syrup, and broth and blend until smooth. Stir the tamarind mixture into the vegetables, along with the chili powder, coriander, cumin, and salt and pepper. Bring to boil, then reduce the heat to medium and simmer, covered, until the potatoes are tender for about 40 minutes.

2. **Finish and Serve**

Taste, adjusting seasonings if necessary, and stir in the peas. Simmer, uncovered, for another 10 minutes. Serve immediately.

Cream Of Artichoke Soup

Prep: 10 Minutes • Cook Time: 20 Minutes • Total: 30 Minutes • Serves: 4 Servings

Ingredients

1 tablespoon extra-virgin olive oil

2 medium shallots, chopped

2 (10-ounce) packages frozen artichoke hearts, thawed

3 cups vegetable broth, homemade or water

1 teaspoon fresh lemon juice

Salt

⅓ cup almond butter

⅛ teaspoon ground cayenne

1 cup plain unsweetened soy milk

1 tablespoon snipped fresh chives, for garnish

2 tablespoons sliced toasted almonds, for garnish

Directions

1. **Preparing the Ingredients**

In a large soup pot, heat the oil over medium heat. Add the shallots, cover, and cook until softened. Uncover and stir in the artichoke hearts, broth, lemon juice, and salt. Bring to a boil, then reduce heat to low and simmer, uncovered, until the artichokes are tender for about 20 minutes.

Add the almond butter and cayenne to the artichoke mixture.

2. Finish and Serve

Purée in a high-speed blender or food processor, in batches if necessary, then return to the pot. Stir in the soy milk, taste and adjust seasonings if necessary. Simmer the soup over medium heat until hot.

Ladle into bowls, sprinkle with chives and almonds, then serve.

Pomegranate-Infused Lentil And Chickpea Stew

Prep: 5 Minutes • Cook Time: 55 Minutes • Total: 60 Minutes • Serves: 4 Servings

Ingredients

¾ cup brown lentils, picked over, rinsed, and drained

2 tablespoons extra-virgin olive oil

½cup chopped green onions

2 teaspoons minced fresh ginger

¾ cup long-grain brown rice

½ cup dried apricots, quartered

¼ cup golden raisins

¼ teaspoon ground allspice

¼ teaspoon ground cumin

¼ teaspoon ground cayenne

1 teaspoon turmeric

Salt and freshly ground black pepper

⅓ cup pomegranate molasses, homemade or store-bought

3 cups water

1½ cups cooked or 1 (15.5-ounce) can chickpeas, drained and rinsed

¼ cup minced fresh cilantro or parsley

Directions

1. Preparing the Ingredients

Soak the lentils in a medium bowl of hot water for 45 minutes. Drain and set aside.

In a large saucepan, heat the oil over medium heat. Add the green onions, ginger, soaked lentils, rice, apricots, raisins, allspice, cumin, cayenne, turmeric, and salt and pepper. Cook and stir for 1 minute.

Add the pomegranate molasses and water, then bring to boil. Reduce heat to low. Cover and simmer until the lentils and rice are tender for about 40 minutes.

2. Finish and Serve

Stir in the chickpeas and cilantro. Simmer, uncovered, for 15 minutes to heat through and allow the flavors to blend. Serve immediately

Rice And Pea Soup

Prep: 5 Minutes • Cook Time: 45 Minutes • Total: 50

Minutes • Serves: 4 Servings

Ingredients

2 tablespoons extra-virgin olive oil

1 medium onion, minced

2 garlic cloves minced

1 cup Arborio rice

6 cups vegetable broth or water

Salt and freshly ground black pepper

1 (16-ounce) bag frozen petite green peas

¼ cup chopped fresh flat-leaf parsley

Directions

1.　Preparing the Ingredients

In a large soup pot, heat the oil over medium heat. Add the onion and garlic, cover, and cook until softened for about 5 minutes.

Uncover and add the rice, broth, and salt and pepper. Bring to boil, then reduce heat to low. Cover and simmer until the rice begins to soften for about 30 minutes.

2.　Finish and serve

Stir in the peas and cook, uncovered, for 15 to 20 minutes. Stir in the parsley and serve

Ethiopian Cabbage, Carrot, and Potato Stew

Prep: 10 Minutes • Cook Time: 20 Minutes • Total: 30

Minutes • Serves: 6

Ingredients

3 russet potatoes, peeled and cut into ½-inch cubes

2 tablespoons extra-virgin olive oil

6 carrots, peeled, halved lengthwise, and cut into ½-inch slices

1 onion, chopped

4 garlic cloves, minced

1 tablespoon ground turmeric

1 teaspoon ground cumin

1 teaspoon ground ginger

1½ teaspoons sea salt

1½ cups low-sodium vegetable broth, divided

4 cups shredded or thinly sliced green cabbage

Directions

1.　Preparing the Ingredients

Bring a large pot of water to boil over medium-high heat. Add the potatoes and cook for 10 minutes, or until fork-tender. Drain and set aside. While the potatoes are cooking, heat the oil in a large skillet over medium-high heat. Add the carrots and onion, then sauté for 5 minutes. Add the garlic, turmeric, cumin, ginger, and salt, then sauté for 1 additional minute until fragrant. Add the cooked potatoes and 1 cup of broth to the skillet, bring to a boil, and reduce to a simmer. Scatter the cabbage on top of the potatoes. Cover and simmer for 3 minutes.

Mix the cabbage into the potatoes, add the remaining ½ cup of broth, cover, and simmer for 5 more minutes, or until the cabbage is wilted and tender.

2. Finish and Serve

Stir the cabbage from time to time while cooking to incorporate it with the other ingredients as it continues to wilt.

Thai-Inspired Coconut Soup

Prep: 5 Minutes • Cook Time: 25 Minutes • Total: 30 Minutes • Serves: 4 Servings

Ingredients

1 tablespoon canola or grapeseed oil

1 medium onion, chopped

2 tablespoons minced fresh ginger

2 tablespoons soy sauce

1 tablespoon light brown sugar (optional)

1 teaspoon Asian chili paste

2½ cups light vegetable broth or water

8 ounces extra-firm tofu, drained and cut into ½-inch dice

2 (13.5-ounce) cans unsweetened coconut milk

1 tablespoon fresh lime juice

3 tablespoons chopped fresh cilantro, for garnish

Directions

1. Preparing the Ingredients

In a large soup pot, heat the oil over medium heat. Add the onion and ginger and cook until softened for about 5 minutes. Stir in the soy sauce, sugar, and chile paste. Add the broth and bring to boil. Reduce heat to medium and simmer for 15 minutes.

Strain the broth and discard solids. Return the broth to the pot over medium heat. Add the tofu and stir in the coconut milk and lime juice. Simmer for 5 minutes longer to allow flavors to blend.

2. Finish and Serve

Ladle into bowls, sprinkle with cilantro, then serve.

Curried Butternut And Red Lentil Soup With Chard

Prep: 5 Minutes • Cook Time: 55 Minutes • Total: 60 Minutes • Serves: 4 Servings

Ingredients

1 tablespoon extra-virgin olive oil

1 medium onion, chopped

1 medium butternut squash, peeled and diced

1 garlic clove, minced

1 tablespoon minced fresh ginger

1 tablespoon hot or mild curry powder

1 (14.5-ounce) can crushed tomatoes

1 cup red lentils, picked over, rinsed, and drained

5 cups vegetable broth, homemade (see Light Vegetable Broth) or store-bought, or water

Salt and freshly ground black pepper

3 cups chopped stemmed Swiss chard

Directions

1. Preparing the Ingredients

In a large soup pot, heat the oil over medium heat. Add the onion, squash, and garlic. Cover and cook until softened for about 10 minutes.

Stir in the ginger and curry powder, then add the tomatoes, lentils, broth, and salt and pepper. Bring to boil, then reduce heat to low and simmer, uncovered, until the lentils and vegetables are tender. Stir occasionally for about 45 minutes.

2. Finish and serve

About 15 minutes before serving, stir in the chard. Taste and adjust seasonings if necessary, then serve.

Spinach, Walnut, And Apple Soup

Prep: 10 Minutes • Cook Time: 20 Minutes • Total: 30 Minutes • Serves: 4 Servings

Ingredients

1 tablespoon extra-virgin olive oil

1 small onion, chopped

3 cups vegetable broth, homemade or store-bought, or water

2 Fuji or other flavorful apples

1 cup apple juice

4 cups fresh spinach

¾ cup ground walnuts

1 teaspoon minced fresh sage or ½teaspoon dried

¼ teaspoon ground allspice

Salt and freshly ground black pepper

1 cup soy milk

¼ cup toasted walnut pieces

Directions

1. Preparing the Ingredients

In a large soup pot, heat the oil over medium heat. Add the onion, cover, and cook until softened for 5 minutes. Add about 1 cup of the vegetable broth, cover, and cook until the onion is very soft for another 5 minutes.

Peel, core, and chop one of the apples, then add it to the pot with the onion and broth. Add the apple juice, spinach, ground walnuts, sage, allspice, with the remaining 2 cups broth, and salt and pepper. Bring to boil, then reduce heat to low and simmer for 10 minutes.

Purée the soup in the pot with an immersion blender or food processor, in batches if necessary, and return to the pot. Stir in the soy milk and reheat over medium heat until hot.

2. Finish and serve

Chop the remaining apple. Ladle the soup into bowls, garnish each bowl with some of the chopped apple, sprinkle with the walnut pieces, then serve.

Tomato Orzo Soup

Prep: 5 Minutes • Cook Time: 30 Minutes • Total: 35 Minutes • Serves: 4 Servings

Ingredients

1 tablespoon extra-virgin olive oil

1 medium onion, chopped

1 celery rib, minced

3 garlic cloves, minced

1 (28-ounce) can crushed tomatoes

3 cups chopped fresh ripe tomatoes

2 tablespoons tomato paste

3 cups vegetable broth, homemade or water

2 bay leaves

Salt and freshly ground black pepper

1 cup plain unsweetened soy milk

1½ cups cooked orzo

2 tablespoons chopped fresh basil, for garnish

Directions

1. Preparing the Ingredients

In a large soup pot, heat the oil over medium heat. Add the onion, celery, and garlic. Cover and cook until softened for about 5 minutes. Stir in the canned and fresh tomatoes, tomato paste, broth, sugar, and bay leaves. Season with salt and pepper and bring to boil. Reduce the heat to low, cover and simmer, until the vegetables are tender for about 20 minutes.

2. Finish and Serve

Remove and discard bay leaves. Purée the soup in the pot with an immersion blender or food processor, in batches if necessary, and return to the pot. Stir in the soy milk, taste and adjust the seasonings if necessary, then heat through.

Spoon about ⅓cup of the orzo into the bottom of each bowl, ladle the hot soup on top, then serve sprinkled with the basil.

Golden Potato Soup

Prep: 5 Minutes • Cook Time: 30 Minutes • Total: 35 Minutes • Serves: 4 To 6 Servings

Ingredients

1 tablespoon extra-virgin olive oil

3 medium shallots, chopped

4 cups vegetable broth, homemade or store-bought, or water

3 medium russet potatoes, peeled and diced

2 medium sweet potatoes, peeled and diced

1 cup plain unsweetened soy milk

Salt and freshly ground black pepper

1 tablespoon minced chives, for garnish

Directions

1. **Preparing the Ingredients**

In a large saucepan, heat the oil over medium heat. Add the shallots, cover, and cook until softened for about 5 minutes. Add the broth and potatoes, then bring to boil. Reduce heat to low and simmer, uncovered, until the potatoes are soft for about 20 minutes.

2. **Finish and Serve**

Purée the potato mixture in the pot with an immersion blender or food processor, in batches if necessary, and return to the pot. Stir in the soy milk and season with salt and pepper. Simmer for 5 minutes to heat through and blend flavors.

Ladle the soup into bowls, sprinkle with chives, then serve.

BEANS AND GRAINS

Red Pepper Lentils

Prep: 5 Minutes • Cook Time: 20 Minutes • Total: 25 Minutes • Serves: 4

Ingredients

1 teaspoon extra-virgin olive oil or canola oil or 2 teaspoons water or vegetable broth

2 teaspoons minced garlic (about 2 cloves)

2 teaspoons grated fresh ginger

½ teaspoon ground cumin

½ teaspoon fennel seeds

1 large red bell pepper, seeded and chopped

1 large tomato, chopped

1 cup dried red lentils

2¼ cups water

2 tablespoons lemon juice (about 1 small lemon)

Directions

1.   Preparing the Ingredients

In a large pot over medium-high heat, heat the olive oil. Add the garlic and ginger, then sauté for 3 minutes, stirring frequently to keep the garlic from sticking.

Add the cumin, fennel, red bell pepper, tomato, lentils, and water. Bring to boil, cover, and reduce the heat to medium-low or low to simmer until the lentils are tender for about 15 minutes. Remove from the heat, then stir in the lemon juice.

2.   Finish and Serve

Transfer to a large storage container, or scoop ½ cup of lentils into each of 4 storage containers. Let it cool before sealing the lids.

Place the airtight containers in the refrigerator for up to 5 days, or freeze for up to 3 months. To thaw, refrigerate overnight. Reheat in the microwave for 1½-3 minutes.

Per Serving: Calories: 206; Fat: 2g; Protein: 13g; Carbohydrates: 34g; Fiber: 16g; Sugar: 4g; Sodium: 9mg

Wild Rice And Millet Croquettes

Prep: 5 Minutes • Cook Time: 20 Minutes • Total: 25 Minutes • Serves: 4 To 6 Servings

Ingredients

¾ cup cooked millet

½ cup cooked wild rice

3 tablespoons extra-virgin olive oil

¼ cup minced onion

1 celery rib, finely minced

¼ cup finely shredded carrot

⅓ cup all-purpose flour

¼ cup chopped fresh parsley

2 teaspoons dried dillweed

Salt and freshly ground black pepper

Directions

1.   Preparing the Ingredients

Place the cooked millet and wild rice in a large bowl and set aside.

In a medium skillet, heat 1 tablespoon of the oil over medium heat. Add the onion, celery, and carrot. Cover and cook until softened for about 5 minutes. Add the vegetables to the cooked grains. Stir in the flour, parsley, dillweed, and salt and pepper. Mix until well combined. Refrigerate until chilled for about 20 minutes.

2.   Cook

Use your hands to shape the mixture into small patties and set aside. In a large skillet, heat the remaining 2 tablespoons oil over medium heat. Add the croquettes and cook until golden brown, turning once, for about 8 minutes in total.

Serve immediately

Caribbean Rice, Squash, And Peas

Prep: 5 Minutes • Cook Time: 40 Minutes • Total: 45 Minutes • Serves: 4 Servings

Ingredients

2 tablespoons extra-virgin olive oil

1 small yellow onion, chopped

2 cups peeled, seeded, and diced butternut or other winter squash

3 garlic cloves, minced

1 teaspoon dried thyme

½ teaspoon ground cumin

1½ cups cooked or 1 (15.5-ounce) can black-eyed peas, drained and rinsed

1 cup long-grain rice

2½ cups hot water

2 tablespoons chopped fresh cilantro

Directions

1.   Preparing the Ingredients

In a large saucepan, heat the oil over medium heat. Add the onion, cover, then cook until softened for about 5 minutes. Add the squash, garlic, thyme, and cumin. Cover and cook until the squash is softened for about 10 minutes. Stir in the peas, rice, and water.

Bring to boil, then reduce heat to low. Cover and simmer until the rice is cooked for about 30 minutes.

2.   Finish and Serve

Fluff with a fork and sprinkle with cilantro. Serve immediately.

Green Tea Rice With Lemon Snow Peas And Tofu

Prep: 7 Minutes • Cook Time: 30 Minutes • Total: 37 Minutes • Serves: 4 Servings

Ingredients

3 cups water

4 green tea bags

1½ cups white sushi rice

2 tablespoons canola or grapeseed oil

8 ounces extra-firm tofu, drained and cut into ¼-inch dice

3 green onions, minced

2 cups snow peas, trimmed and cut diagonally into 1-inch pieces

1 tablespoon fresh lemon juice

1 teaspoon grated lemon zest

Salt and freshly ground black pepper

Directions

1. Preparing the Ingredients

In a large saucepan, bring the water to a boil. Add the tea bags and remove from the heat. Let stand for 7 minutes and remove and discard the tea bags. Rinse the rice under running water until the water runs clear, then add to the brewed tea.

2. Cook

Cover and cook over medium heat until tender, about 25 minutes. Remove from heat and set aside.

In a large skillet, heat the oil over medium heat. Add the tofu and cook until golden brown, 5 minutes. Add the green onions and snow peas and cook until softened, 3 minutes. Stir in the lemon juice and zest.

In a large bowl, combine the cooked rice with the tofu and snow pea mixture.

3. Finish and Serve

Season with salt and pepper to taste, and serve immediately.

Brown Rice And Lentil Pilaf

Prep: 15 Minutes • Cook Time: 50 Minutes • Total: 65 Minutes • Serves: 4 To 6 Servings

Ingredients

1 tablespoon extra-virgin olive oil

1 large yellow onion, minced

1 medium carrot, chopped

2 garlic cloves, minced

1 cup long-grain brown rice

1½ teaspoons ground coriander

½ teaspoon ground cumin

3 cups water

Salt

3 tablespoons minced fresh cilantro

Freshly ground black pepper

Directions

1. Preparing the Ingredients

Bring a saucepan of salted water to boil over high heat. Add the lentils, return to a boil, then reduce heat to medium and cook for 15 minutes. Drain and set aside. In a large saucepan, heat the oil over medium heat. Add the onion, carrot, and garlic, cover, then cook until tender for about 10 minutes.

Add the lentils to the vegetable mixture. Add the rice, coriander, and cumin. Stir in the water and bring to boil. Reduce heat to low, salt the water, and cook, covered, until the lentils and rice are tender for about 30 minutes.

2. Finish and Serve

Remove from heat and set aside for 10 minutes.

Transfer to a large bowl, fluff with a fork, then sprinkle with the cilantro and freshly ground black pepper. Serve immediately.

Mexican Green Rice And Beans

Prep: 10 Minutes • Cook Time: 40 Minutes • Total: 50 Minutes • Serves: 4 Servings

Ingredients

1 large green bell pepper

2 or 3 small fresh jalapeño or other hot green chiles

2½ cups vegetable broth

½ cup coarsely chopped fresh parsley

1 small yellow onion, chopped

2 garlic cloves, chopped

¼ teaspoon freshly ground black pepper

1 teaspoon sugar

½ teaspoon dried oregano

¼ teaspoon ground cumin

3 tablespoons canola or grapeseed oil

1 cup long-grain white rice

Salt

1½ cups cooked or 1 (15.5-ounce) can dark red kidney beans, drained and rinsed

2 tablespoons minced fresh cilantro, garnish

Directions

1. Preparing the Ingredients

Roast the bell pepper and chiles over a gas flame, or under a broiler until the skin blisters, turning on all sides. Place in a paper bag for 5 minutes. Use a damp towel to rub off scorched bits of skin. Stem, seed, and chop the bell pepper and chiles, then place them in a food processor. Add 1 cup of the broth, parsley, onion, garlic, pepper, sugar, oregano, and cumin, then process until smooth. Set aside.

In a large skillet, heat the oil over medium heat. Add the rice and stir constantly for a few minutes to coat the rice with the oil. Add the pureed vegetables and simmer, stirring occasionally for 5 minutes. Add the remaining 1½ cups broth and bring to boil. Reduce the heat to medium, add salt to taste, cover, and cook until the liquid is absorbed for about 30 minutes.

2.   Finish and Serve

About 10 minutes before being ready to serve, stir in the kidney beans. Garnish with cilantro and serve immediately.

Balsamic Black Beans

Prep: 5 Minutes • Cook Time: 20 Minutes • Total: 25 Minutes • Serves: 5

Ingredients

1 teaspoon extra-virgin olive oil or vegetable broth

½ cup diced sweet onion

1 teaspoon ground cumin

1 teaspoon ground cardamom (optional)

2 (14.5-ounce) cans black beans, rinsed and drained

¼ to ½ cup vegetable broth

2 tablespoons balsamic vinegar

Directions

1.   Preparing the Ingredients

In a large pot over medium-high heat, heat the olive oil. Add the onion, cumin, and cardamom (if using) and sauté for 3-5 minutes until the onion is translucent. Add

the beans and ¼ cup broth, then bring to boil. Add up to ½ cup more of broth for "soupier" beans.

Cover, reduce the heat, then simmer for 10 minutes.

Add the balsamic vinegar, increase the heat to medium-high, and cook for 3 more minutes uncovered.

2.   Finish and Serve

Transfer to a large storage container, or divide the beans evenly among 5 single-serving storage containers. Let it cool before sealing the lids.

Place the airtight containers in the refrigerator for up to 5 days, or freeze for up to 2 months. To thaw, refrigerate overnight. Reheat in the microwave for 1½-3 minutes.

Per Serving: Calories: 200; Fat: 2g; Protein: 13g; Carbohydrates: 34g; Fiber: 12g; Sugar: 1g; Sodium: 41mg

Savory Beans And Rice

Prep: 5 Minutes • Cook Time: 40 Minutes • Total: 55 Minutes • Serves: 4 Servings

Ingredients

1 tablespoon extra-virgin olive oil

3 green onions, chopped

1 teaspoon grated fresh ginger

1 cup brown basmati rice

2 cups water

1 tablespoon soy sauce

Pinch of salt

1½ cups cooked or 1 (15.5-ounce) can Great Northern white beans, drained and rinsed

1 tablespoon nutritional yeast

1 tablespoon minced fresh savory or 1½ teaspoons dried

Directions

1. **Preparing the Ingredients**

In a large saucepan, heat the oil over medium heat. Add the green onions and ginger, then cook until fragrant for about 1 minute. Add the rice, water, soy sauce, and salt. Cover and bring to boil. Reduce heat to low and simmer, covered, until the rice is tender for about 30 minutes.

2. **Finish and Serve**

Stir in the beans, nutritional yeast, and savory. Cook, uncovered, and stir until heated through and the liquid is absorbed. Serve immediately.

Dilly White Beans

Prep: 5 Minutes • Cook Time: 20 Minutes • Total: 5 Minutes • Serves: 6

Ingredients

1 teaspoon extra-virgin olive oil or ¼ cup vegetable broth

1 small sweet onion, cut into half-moon slices

2 (14.5-ounce) cans great northern beans, rinsed and drained

½ cup vegetable broth

2 teaspoons dried dill

½ teaspoon salt (optional)

¼ teaspoon freshly ground black pepper

Directions

1. **Preparing the Ingredients.**

In a large skillet or wok over medium-high heat, heat the olive oil. Sauté the onion slices for up to 3-5 minutes, or until the onion is translucent.

Add the beans, broth, dill, salt (if using) and pepper. Bring to boil. Reduce the heat to low and simmer, uncovered, for 10 minutes.

2. **Finish and Serve**

Transfer to a large storage container, or scoop ½ cup of beans into each of 6 storage containers. Let it cool before sealing the lids.

Per Serving: Calories: 155; Fat: 1g; Protein: 10g; Carbohydrates: 26g; Fiber: 9g; Sugar: 1g; Sodium: 67mg

Quinoa Pilaf

Prep: 10 Minutes • Cook Time: 15 Minutes • Total: 25 Minutes • Serves: 4

Ingredients

1 cup quinoa

2 cups vegetable stock

¼ cup pine nuts

2 tablespoons extra-virgin olive oil

½ onion, chopped

⅓ cup chopped fresh parsley

sea salt

freshly ground black pepper

Directions

1. Preparing the Ingredients.

In a medium pot, bring the quinoa and vegetable stock to boil over medium-high heat while stirring occasionally. Reduce to a simmer.

Cover and cook until the quinoa is soft for about 15 minutes. Meanwhile, heat a large sauté pan over medium-high heat. Add the pine nuts to the dry hot pan and toast, stirring frequently, until the nuts are fragrant for 2-3 minutes. Remove the pine nuts from the pan and set aside.

2. Finish and Serve

Add the olive oil to the same pan and heat until it shimmers. Add the onion and cook until soft for about 5 minutes. When the quinoa is soft and all the liquid is absorbed, remove it from the heat and fluff it with a fork. Stir in the pine nuts, onion, and parsley. Season with salt and pepper. Serve hot.

Five-Spice Farro

Prep: 3 Minutes • Cook Time: 35 Minutes • Total: 38 Minutes • Serves: 4

Ingredients

1 cup dried farro, rinsed and drained

1 teaspoon five-spice powder

Directions

1. Preparing the Ingredients

In a medium pot, combine the farro, five-spice powder, and enough water to cover.

Bring to a boil; reduce the heat to medium-low, and simmer for 30 minutes. Drain off any excess water.

2. Finish and Serve

Transfer to a large storage container, or scoop 1 cup farro into each of 4 storage containers. Let cool before sealing the lids.

Place the airtight containers in the refrigerator for 1 week or freeze for up to 3 months. To thaw, refrigerate overnight. Reheat in the microwave for 1½ to 3 minutes.

Per Serving: Calories: 73; Fat: 0g; Protein: 3g; Carbohydrates: 15g; Fiber: 1g; Sugar: 0g; Sodium: 0mg

Italian Rice With Seitan And Mushrooms

Prep: 15 Minutes • Cook Time: 0 Minutes • Total: 15 Minutes • Serves: 4 Servings

Ingredients

2 cups water

1 cup long-grain brown or white rice

2 tablespoons extra-virgin olive oil

1 medium yellow onion, chopped

2 garlic cloves, minced

8 ounces seitan, homemade or store-bought, chopped

8 ounces white mushrooms, chopped

1 teaspoon dried basil

½ teaspoon ground fennel seed

¼ teaspoon crushed red pepper

Salt and freshly ground black pepper

Directions

1. Preparing the Ingredients

In a large saucepan, bring the water to boil over high heat. Add the rice, reduce the heat to low, cover, and cook until tender, about 30 minutes.

In a large skillet, heat the oil over medium heat. Add the onion, cover, and cook until softened, about 5 minutes. Add the seitan and cook uncovered until browned. Stir in the mushrooms and cook until tender, about 5 minutes longer. Stir in the basil, fennel, crushed red pepper, and salt and black pepper to taste.

2. Finish and Serve

Transfer the cooked rice to large serving bowl. Stir in the seitan mixture and mix thoroughly. Add a generous amount of black pepper and serve immediately.

Stovetop Thanksgiving Rice Stuffing

Prep: 10 Minutes • Cook Time: 15 Minutes • Total: 25 Minutes • Serves: 8

Ingredients

¼ cup vegan butter

1 onion, chopped

2 celery stalks, thinly sliced

1 (8-ounce) package baby bella or white button mushrooms, stemmed and sliced

3 garlic cloves, minced

½ cup low-sodium vegetable broth

½ cup dried cranberries or cherries

½ cup chopped walnuts, toasted

2 cups cooked wild-rice blend or brown rice

1 teaspoon poultry seasoning

1 teaspoon sea salt

Chopped fresh parsley, for garnish

Directions

1. Preparing the Ingredients

Melt the butter in a large skillet over medium heat.

Add the onion, celery, and mushrooms, then sauté for 5 minutes, or until soft. Add the garlic and sauté for 1 additional minute, or until fragrant. Add the broth, cranberries, and walnuts. Bring to boil, cover, reduce the heat, and simmer for 5 minutes, or until fragrant.

2. Finish and Serve

Add the rice, poultry seasoning, and salt, then mix well to combine. Continue to cook, uncovered, for about 4 minutes, stirring occasionally or until heated through and all the liquid evaporates. Transfer to a serving dish and garnish with parsley.

Chipotle Chickpeas (Pressure Cooker)

Prep: 8 Minutes • Pressure: 20 Minutes • Total: 45 Minutes • Pressure Level: High • Release: Natural• Serves 4-6

Ingredients

1 cup dried chickpeas, soaked in water overnight

2 cups water

¼ cup sun-dried tomatoes, chopped

1 to 2 tablespoons extra-virgin olive oil

2 teaspoons ground chipotle pepper

1½ teaspoons ground cumin

1½ teaspoons onion powder

1 teaspoon dried oregano

¾ teaspoon garlic powder

½ teaspoon smoked paprika

¼ to ½ teaspoon salt

Directions

1. **Preparing the Ingredients** Drain and rinse the chickpeas, drain again, and put them into your electric pressure cooker's cooking pot. Add the water, sun-dried tomatoes, olive oil, chipotle pepper, cumin, onion powder, oregano, garlic powder, and paprika.

2. **High pressure for 20 minutes** Lock the lid and ensure the pressure valve is sealed, then select High Pressure and set the time for 20 minutes.

3. **Pressure Release** Once the cook time is complete, let the pressure release naturally for about 15 minutes. Once all the pressure has released, unlock and remove the lid. Taste and season with salt and adding more oil or seasonings if you like.

PER SERVING Calories: 280; Total fat: 7g; Protein: 13g; Sodium: 168mg; Fiber: 12g

GGB Bowl

Prep: 10 Minutes • Cook Time: 5 Minutes • Total: 15 Minutes • Serves: 2

Ingredients

2 teaspoons extra-virgin olive oil

1 cup cooked brown rice, quinoa, or your grain of choice

1 (15-ounce) can chickpeas or your beans of choice, rinsed and drained

1 bunch spinach or kale, stemmed and roughly chopped

1 tablespoon soy sauce or gluten-free tamari

Sea salt

Black pepper

Directions

1. Preparing the Ingredients.

In a large skillet, heat the oil over medium heat.

Add the rice, beans, and greens, then stir continuously until the greens have wilted and everything is heated through for 3-5 minutes.

2. Finish and Serve

Drizzle in the soy sauce, mix to combine, and season with salt and pepper.

Easy Kitchari

Prep: 20 Minutes • Cook Time: 20 Minutes • Total: 40 Minutes • Serves: 5

Ingredients

½ cup yellow mung beans or split peas

½ cup basmati rice

1 small red onion, diced

1 (14.5-ounce) can diced tomatoes

5 teaspoons minced garlic (about 5 cloves)

1 jalapeño, seeded

½ teaspoon ground ginger or 2 tablespoons minced fresh ginger

1 teaspoon ground turmeric

2 tablespoons to ¼ cup water

1 teaspoon extra-virgin olive oil or 1 to 2 tablespoons vegetable broth

1¼ teaspoons ground cumin

1¼ teaspoons ground coriander

1 teaspoon fennel seeds

4 cups chopped vegetables (mix of carrot, cauliflower, summer or winter squash, broccoli, and/or potatoes)

3 cups water

Juice of 1 large lemon

1 2 teaspoons salt, to taste

½ teaspoon freshly ground black pepper

Directions

1. Preparing the Ingredients.

Rinse and drain the beans and rice. Transfer to a small bowl and soak in water for 15 minutes.

In a food processor or blender, purée the onion, tomatoes with their juices, garlic, jalapeño, ginger, turmeric, and 2 tablespoons of water, adding water as necessary, until you reach a sauce consistency that pours easily and is not chunky.

In a large pot over medium-high heat, heat the olive oil. Add the cumin, coriander, and fennel seeds then sauté, stirring constantly until fragrant.

Transfer the purée to the pot. Drain and rinse the soaked rice and beans, then add them to the pot. Add the chopped vegetables and water to combine well.

Bring to boil. Cover, reduce the heat to low, and simmer for 15-20 minutes until the beans and rice are soft but not mushy.

2. Finish and Serve

Add the lemon juice, and taste before adding the salt and pepper. Into each of 5 single-serving storage containers, spoon 2 cups.

Per Serving: Calories: 234; Fat: 3g; Protein: 7g; Carbohydrates: 47g; Fiber: 13g; Sugar: 5g; Sodium: 862mg

Chickpea and Artichoke Curry

Prep: 10 Minutes • Cook Time: 15 Minutes • Total: 25 Minutes • Serves: 4

Ingredients

1 teaspoon extra-virgin olive oil or 2 teaspoons vegetable broth

1 small onion, diced

2 teaspoons minced garlic (2 cloves)

1 (14.5-ounce) can chickpeas, rinsed and drained

1 (14.5-ounce) can artichoke hearts, drained and quartered

2 teaspoons curry powder

½ teaspoon ground coriander

½ teaspoon ground cumin

1 (5.4-ounce) can unsweetened coconut milk

Directions

Preparing the Ingredients.

1.   In a large skillet or pot over medium-high heat, heat the olive oil. Add the onion and garlic, then sauté for about 5 minutes. Add the chickpeas, artichoke hearts, curry powder, coriander, and cumin. Stir to combine well. Pour the coconut milk into the pot, mix well, and bring to a boil. Cover, reduce the heat to low, and simmer for 10 minutes.

2.   Finish and Serve

Divide the curry evenly among 4 wide-mouth glass jars or single-compartment containers. Let cool it before sealing the lids.

Per Serving: Calories: 267; Fat: 12g; Protein: 9g; Carbohydrates: 36g; Fiber: 11g; Sugar: 3g; Sodium: 373mg

Curried Lentils (Pressure cooker)

Prep: 6 Minutes • Pressure: 20 Minutes • Total: 60 Minutes • Pressure Level: High • Release: Natural• Serves 6-8

Ingredients

1 tablespoon coconut oil

2 tablespoons mild curry powder

1 teaspoon ground ginger

½ teaspoon ground turmeric (optional)

1 cup dried green lentils or brown lentils

3 cups water

1 teaspoon freshly squeezed lime juice (optional)

½ teaspoon salt

Freshly ground black pepper (optional)

Directions

1. **Preparing the Ingredients.** On your electric pressure cooker, select Sauté. Add the coconut oil, curry powder, ginger, and turmeric (if using) and toss to toast for 1 minute. Add the lentils and toss with the spices. Add the water. Cancel Sauté.

2. **High pressure for 20 minutes.** Close and lock the lid, ensuring the pressure valve is sealed, then select High Pressure and set the time for 20 minutes.

3. **Pressure Release.** Once the cook time is complete, let the pressure release naturally, about 30 minutes. Once all the pressure has released, carefully unlock and remove the lid. Stir in the lime juice (if using). Season with the salt and pepper, if you like.

PER SERVING Calories: 212; Total fat: 5g; Protein: 13g; Sodium: 2mg; Fiber: 16g

Pesto Pearled Barley

Prep: 1 Minute • Cook Time: 50 Minutes • Total: 51 Minutes • Serves: 4

Ingredients

1 cup dried barley

2½ cups vegetable broth

½ cup Parm-y Kale Pesto

Directions

1. **Preparing the Ingredients.**

In a medium saucepan, combine the barley and broth, then bring to boil.

Cover, reduce the heat to low, and simmer for about 45 minutes until tender.

Remove from the stove and let it stand for 5 minutes.

2. **Finish and Serve**

Fluff the barley, then gently fold in the pesto.

Scoop about ¾ cup into each of 4 single-compartment storage containers. Let it cool before sealing the lids.

Per Serving: Calories: 237; Fat: 6g; Protein: 9g; Carbohydrates: 40g; Fiber: 11g; Sugar: 2g; Sodium: 365mg

Spicy Picnic Beans

Prep: 15 Minutes • Cook Time: 15 Minutes • Total: 30 Minutes • Serves: 6

Ingredients

1 jalapeño, cut into strips

1 red bell pepper, cut into strips

1 green bell pepper, cut into strips

1 onion, chopped

5 garlic cloves, minced

two 15-ounce cans pinto beans, drained and rinsed

one 15-ounce can kidney beans, drained and rinsed

one 15-ounce can chickpeas, drained and rinsed

one 18-ounce bottle barbecue sauce

½ teaspoon chipotle powder

sea salt

freshly ground black pepper

Directions

1. Preparing the Ingredients

In the bowl of a food processor, combine the jalapeño, bell peppers, onion, and garlic, then blend for ten 1-second pulses, stopping halfway through to scrape down the sides of the bowl. In a large pot, combine the processed mixture with the beans, barbecue sauce, and chipotle powder.

Simmer over medium-high heat, stirring frequently to blend the flavors for about 15 minutes.

2. Finish and Serve

Season with salt and pepper. Serve hot. You can make this ahead of time and store it in a tightly sealed container for up to 3 days in the refrigerator. The flavors will blend and deepen as the beans rest.

Peas and Pesto Rice

Prep: 5 Minutes • Cook Time: 5 Minutes • Total: 10 Minutes • Serves: 3

Ingredients

1 cup Pistachio Pesto or store bought vegan pesto

1 cup frozen peas, thawed

2 cups cooked brown rice

Directions

1. Preparing the Ingredients.

In a large skillet, warm the pesto sauce and peas over low heat for 3 to 5 minutes, until heated through. Add the rice and mix until everything is coated.

Cinnamon Chickpeas (Pressure Cooker)

Prep: 12 Minutes • Pressure: 30 Minutes • Total: 50 Minutes • Pressure Level: High • Release: Natural• Serves 4-6

Ingredients

1 cup dried chickpeas, soaked in water overnight

2 cups water

2 teaspoons ground cinnamon, plus more as needed

½ teaspoon ground nutmeg (optional)

1 tablespoon coconut oil

2 to 4 tablespoons unrefined sugar or brown sugar, plus more as needed

Directions

1. **Preparing the Ingredients.** Drain and rinse the chickpeas, then put them in your electric pressure cooker's cooking pot. Add the water, cinnamon, and nutmeg (if using).

2. **High pressure for 30 minutes.** Lock the lid and ensure the pressure valve is sealed, then select High Pressure and set the time for 30 minutes.

3. **Pressure Release.** Once the cook time is complete, let the pressure release naturally for about 15 minutes. Once all the pressure has released, unlock and remove the lid. Drain any excess water from the chickpeas and add them back to the pot. Stir in the coconut oil and sugar. Taste and add more cinnamon, if desired.

Select Sauté and cook for about 5 minutes, stirring the chickpeas occasionally, until there's no liquid left and the sugar has melted onto the chickpeas. Transfer to a bowl and toss with additional sugar if you want to add a crunchy texture.

PER SERVING Calories: 253; Total fat: 7g; Protein: 11g; Sodium: 9mg; Fiber: 10g

Lentil Spinach Curry

Prep: 5 Minutes • Cook Time: 30 Minutes • Total: 35 Minutes • Serves: 4

Ingredients

1 teaspoon extra-virgin olive oil

1 onion, chopped

½-inch piece fresh ginger, peeled and minced

1 to 2 tablespoons mild curry powder

1½ cups dried green or brown lentils

2½ cups water or Vegetable Broth

1 cup canned diced tomatoes

2 to 4 cups finely chopped raw spinach

½ cup nondairy milk

2 tablespoons soy sauce (optional)

1 tablespoon apple cider vinegar or rice vinegar

1 teaspoon salt (or 2 teaspoons if omitting soy sauce)

Directions

1. **Preparing the Ingredients.**

Heat the olive oil in a large pot over medium heat. Add the onion, and sauté for about 3 minutes until soft.

Add the ginger, and cook for 1 minute. Stir in the curry powder, lentils, and water. Bring to boil, turn the heat to low, and cover the pot. Simmer for about 15-20 minutes until the lentils are soft. Stir in the tomatoes, spinach, milk, soy sauce (if using), vinegar, and salt. Simmer for about 3 minutes until heated through. If you prefer, use an immersion blender to half-blend this in the pot for a creamier texture and to hide the spinach.

2. **Finish and Serve**

Store in an airtight container for 4-5 days in the refrigerator, or up to 1 month in the freezer.

Per Serving Calories: 313; Protein: 21g; Total fat: 3g; Saturated fat: 0g; Carbohydrates: 52g; Fiber: 24g

White Bean Burgers

Prep: 10 Minutes • Cook Time: 10 Minutes • Total: 20 Minutes • Serves: 4

Ingredients

1 tablespoon extra-virgin olive oil, plus more for coating the baking sheet

¼ cup couscous

¼ cup boiling water

1 (15-ounce) can white beans, drained and rinsed

2 tablespoons balsamic vinegar

2 tablespoons chopped sun-dried tomatoes or olives

½ teaspoon garlic powder or 1 garlic clove, finely minced

½ teaspoon salt

4 burger buns

Lettuce leaves, for serving

Tomato slices, for serving

Condiments of choice, such as ketchup, olive tapenade, *Creamy Tahini Dressing*, and/or *Spinach Pesto*

Directions

1.   Preparing the Ingredients.

If baking, preheat the oven to 350°F. Coat a rimmed baking sheet with olive oil, or line it with parchment paper or a silicone mat. In a medium heat-proof bowl, combine the couscous and boiling water.

Cover and set aside for about 5 minutes. Once the couscous is soft and the water is absorbed, fluff it with a fork. Add the beans, and mash them to a chunky texture. Add the vinegar, olive oil, sun-dried tomatoes, garlic powder, and salt; stir until combined but still a bit chunky. Divide the mixture into 4 portions, and shape each into a patty. Put the patties on the prepared baking sheet, and bake for 25-30 minutes until slightly crispy on the edges. Alternatively, heat some olive oil in a large skillet over medium heat, then add the patties, making sure each has oil under it. Fry for about 5 minutes until the bottoms are browned. Flip, adding more oil as needed, and fry for an extra 5 minutes.

2.   Finish and Serve

Serve the burgers on buns with lettuce, tomato, and your choice of condiments.

Chickpeas with Lemon and Spinach

Prep: 10 Minutes • Cook Time: 10 Minutes • Total: 20 Minutes • Serves: 4

Ingredients

3 tablespoons extra-virgin olive oil

one 15-ounce can chickpeas, drained and rinsed

10 ounces baby spinach

½ teaspoon sea salt

juice and zest of 1 lemon

freshly ground black pepper

Directions

1. **Preparing the Ingredients.**

In a large sauté pan, heat the olive oil over medium-high heat until it shimmers. Add the chickpeas and cook until they are heated through, about 5 minutes.

Add the spinach and stir just until it wilts, about 5 minutes.

2. **Finish and Serve**

Add the salt, lemon juice, lemon zest, and pepper and stir to combine. Serve immediately.

VEGETABLES

Broccoli And White Beans With Potatoes And Walnuts

Prep: 5 Minutes • Cook Time: 35 Minutes • Total: 40 Minutes • Serves: 4 Servings

Ingredients

1½ pounds fingerling potatoes

4 cups broccoli florets

3 tablespoons extra-virgin olive oil

3 garlic cloves, minced

¾ cup chopped walnut pieces

¼ teaspoon crushed red pepper

1½ cups or 1 (15.5-ounce) can white beans, drained and rinsed

1 teaspoon dried savory

Salt and freshly ground black pepper

1 tablespoon fresh lemon juice

Directions

1.   Preparing the Ingredients

Steam the potatoes until tender for about 20 minutes. Set aside.

Steam the broccoli until crisp-tender. Set aside.

In a large skillet, heat 2 tablespoons of the oil over medium heat. Add the garlic, walnuts, and crushed red pepper. Cook until the garlic is softened.

Stir in the steamed potatoes and broccoli. Add the beans and savory, then season with salt and black pepper. Cook until heated through.

2.   Finish and Serve

Sprinkle with lemon juice and drizzle with the remaining 1 tablespoon olive oil.

Serve immediately.

Bell Peppers Stuffed With White Beans And Mushrooms

Prep: 5 Minutes • Cook Time: 40 Minutes • Total: 45 Minutes • Serves: 4 Servings

Ingredients

2 large or 4 small red or yellow bell peppers

2 tablespoons extra-virgin olive oil

1 small yellow onion, minced

2 garlic cloves, minced

12 ounces white mushrooms, lightly rinsed, patted dry, and chopped

3 cups cooked or 2 (15.5-ounce) cans white beans, drained, rinsed, and mashed

1 cup finely chopped walnuts

2 tablespoons minced fresh parsley or dillweed

½cup dry unseasoned bread crumbs

Salt and freshly ground black pepper

Directions

1. **Preparing the Ingredients**

Cut the bell peppers in half lengthwise and remove the seeds and membranes. Cook the peppers in a pot of boiling water to soften. Drain and set aside.

Preheat the oven to 375°F. Lightly oil a 9 x 13-inch baking pan and set aside.

In a large skillet, heat the oil over medium heat. Add the onion, cover, and cook until softened. Add the garlic and mushrooms and cook, uncovered, for 5 minutes. Add the beans, walnuts, parsley, and ¼ cup of the bread crumbs to the mushroom mixture. Season with salt and black pepper and mix well.

Stuff the softened pepper halves with the enough of the stuffing mixture to fill the peppers (½-1 cup, depending on the size of the pepper) and arrange stuffing side up in the prepared baking pan.

2. **Bake**

Cover with foil and bake for 20 minutes. Uncover, sprinkle with the remaining bread crumbs, and continue baking until the peppers are hot and the crumbs are golden brown. Serve immediately.

Roasted Rosemary Potatoes

Prep: 5 Minutes • Cook Time: 30 Minutes • Total: 35 Minutes • Serves: 4

Ingredients

1½ pounds baby red potatoes, halved

2 tablespoons extra-virgin olive oil

3 garlic cloves, minced

1 tablespoon minced fresh rosemary

¾ teaspoon sea salt

Directions

1. **Preparing the Ingredients.**

Preheat the oven to 425°F. Line a baking sheet with parchment paper.

In a large bowl, toss the potatoes with the oil, garlic, rosemary, and salt until well combined.

2. **Bake**

Spread the potatoes evenly on the prepared baking sheet and bake for 15 minutes. Toss with a spatula and bake for an additional 15 minutes, or until golden brown.

Three-Green Tian

Prep: 15 Minutes • Cook Time: 60 Minutes • Total: 75 Minutes • Serves: 4 To 6 Servings

Ingredients

2 medium baking potatoes, cut into ¼-inch slices

3 medium zucchini, cut into 1⁄4-inch slices on the diagonal

3⁄4 cup extra-virgin olive oil

Salt and freshly ground black pepper

1 medium yellow onion, chopped

3 garlic cloves, minced

3 cups packed fresh spinach leaves, tough stems removed and coarsely chopped

2 cups packed stemmed and chopped kale

2 cups stemmed and chopped Swiss chard

1 cup loosely packed fresh basil leaves

5 to 6 ripe plum tomatoes, cut into 1⁄4-inch slices

3⁄4 cup fresh bread crumbs

3 tablespoons vegan Parmesan

Directions

1. **Preparing the Ingredients**

Preheat the oven to 400°F.

Lightly oil a 9 x 13-inch baking pan and set aside.

Lightly oil two large baking sheets and arrange the potato slices on one of them, overlapping as needed. Arrange the zucchini slices on the other, overlapping as needed. Drizzle with 1 or 2 tablespoons of the oil and season with salt and pepper.

Bake the zucchini slices until softened, and the potato slices until softened. Remove from the oven and set aside.

In a large skillet, heat 1 tablespoon of the oil over medium heat. Add the onion and garlic. Cover and cook until softened. Stir in the spinach, kale, and chard and season with salt and pepper. Cover and cook until the greens are wilted.

Transfer the greens mixture to a blender or food processor and process with the basil and 3 tablespoons of the remaining oil until smooth. Season with salt and pepper.

Line the bottom of the prepared pan with a half of the cooked potato slices, overlapping as needed. Spoon a very thin layer of the pureed greens evenly over the potatoes. Arrange a layer of half of the cooked zucchini slices on top, overlapping as needed, followed by more of the puréed greens. Arrange a layer of tomato slices on top, followed by more of the greens. Repeat using the remaining potato, zucchini, and tomato slices and the remaining puréed greens, seasoning each layer with salt and pepper.

2. **Bake**

Cover tightly with foil and bake until the vegetables are tender for about 45 minutes. Remove from the oven and sprinkle the tian with the bread crumbs and Parmesan, then drizzle it with the remaining olive oil. Return to the oven and bake uncovered for 10 minutes to brown the topping. Serve immediately.

Kasha With Roasted Sweet Potatoes And Peas

Prep: 5 Minutes • Cook Time: 50 Minutes • Total: 55 Minutes • Serves: 4 Servings

Ingredients

2 large sweet potatoes, peeled and cut into ½-inch dice

2 tablespoons extra-virgin olive oil

Salt and freshly ground black pepper

1 large yellow onion, finely chopped

1 cup coarse kasha (buckwheat groats)

2 cups vegetable broth or water

1 cup frozen peas

Directions

1. **Preparing the Ingredients**

Preheat the oven to 425°F. Spread the sweet potatoes on a lightly oiled baking pan and drizzle with 1 tablespoon of the oil. Season with salt and pepper and roast until tender for about 25 minutes, while stirring once about halfway through. Set aside.

In a large skillet, heat the remaining 1 tablespoon oil over medium heat. Add the onion, cover, and cook, stirring occasionally, until browned for about 10 minutes. Stir in the kasha. Add the broth and bring to boil. Reduce the heat to low, cover, and simmer until the kasha is cooked.

2. **Finish and Serve**

Add the peas and roasted sweet potatoes and season with salt and pepper. Stir gently to combine. Serve immediately.

Millet, Chard, And White Bean Casserole

Prep: 5 Minutes • Cook Time: 45 Minutes • Total: 50 Minutes • Serves: 4 To 6 Servings

Ingredients

2¾ cups water

1 cup millet

Salt

1 tablespoon extra-virgin olive oil

1 medium yellow onion, chopped

1 medium red bell pepper, chopped

2 garlic cloves, minced

3 cups chopped stemmed Swiss chard

Salt and freshly ground black pepper

1½ cups cooked or 1 (15.5-ounce) can Great Northern beans, drained and rinsed

1 cup ripe cherry tomatoes, quartered

2 tablespoons fresh lemon juice

¼ cup nutritional yeast (optional)

2 tablespoons minced fresh dillweed

2 tablespoons minced fresh parsley

⅓ cup dry unseasoned bread crumbs

Directions

1. Preparing the Ingredients

In a large saucepan, bring the water to boil over high heat. Add the millet and ½ teaspoon of salt and return to boil. Reduce the heat to low, cover, and simmer until tender for 30-40 minutes. Set aside.

Preheat the oven to 350°F. Lightly oil a 2-quart casserole and set aside. In a large skillet, heat the oil over medium heat. Add the onion and bell pepper, cover, and cook until softened. Add the garlic and chard, then season with salt and black pepper. Cover and cook, while stirring occasionally, until the chard is wilted. Stir the chard mixture into the cooked millet, along with the beans, tomatoes, lemon juice, yeast, dillweed, and parsley.

3. Finish and Serve

Transfer the mixture to the prepared casserole and sprinkle evenly with bread crumbs. Bake, uncovered.

Mushroom Goulash

Prep: 5 Minutes • Cook Time: 45 Minutes • Total: 50 Minutes • Serves: 4 Servings

Ingredients

1 tablespoon extra-virgin olive oil

1 large yellow onion, chopped

3 garlic cloves, minced

1 large russet potato, cut into ½-inch dice

4 large portobello mushrooms, lightly rinsed, patted dry, and cut into 1-inch chunks

1 tablespoon tomato paste

½ cup dry white wine

1½ tablespoons sweet Hungarian paprika

1 teaspoon caraway seeds

1½ cups fresh or canned sauerkraut, drained

1½ cups vegetable broth

Salt and freshly ground black pepper

½ cup vegan sour cream

Directions

1. Preparing the Ingredients

In large saucepan, heat the oil over medium heat. Add the onion, garlic, and potato. Cover and cook until softened for about 10 minutes. Add the mushrooms and cook, uncovered, 3 minutes longer. Stir in the tomato paste, wine, paprika, caraway seeds, and sauerkraut. Add the broth and bring to boil, then reduce heat to low and season with salt and pepper. Cover and simmer until the vegetables are soft and the flavor is developed for about 30 minutes.

2. Finish and Serve

Spoon about 1 cup of liquid into a small bowl. Add the sour cream, stirring to blend. Stir the sour cream mixture back into the saucepan and taste, adjusting the seasonings if necessary.

Serve immediately.

Tamarind Eggplant With Bell Peppers And Mango

Prep: 5 Minutes • Cook Time: 35 Minutes • Total: 40 Minutes • Serves: 4 Servings

Ingredients

½ cup extra-virgin olive oil

1 medium yellow onion, cut into ½-inch dice

3 small Asian eggplants, peeled and cut into 1-inch chunks

1 medium red pepper, cut into ½-inch dice

1 medium yellow bell pepper, cut into ½-inch dice

3 garlic cloves, minced

1 serrano or other small hot chile, seeded and minced

2 tablespoons tamarind paste

½ cup fresh orange juice

2 teaspoons light brown sugar

Salt and freshly ground black pepper

1 ripe mango, peeled, pitted, and cut into ½-inch dice

½ cup finely chopped fresh cilantro

Directions

1. Preparing the Ingredients

In a large skillet, heat the oil over medium heat. Add the onion, cover, and cook until softened. Add the eggplants, red and yellow bell peppers, garlic, and chile. Cook, covered, until softened.

Add the tamarind paste, orange juice, sugar, and salt and black pepper. Bring to boil, then reduce heat to low and simmer, uncovered, until the vegetables are soft and the liquid thickens and reduces by half for about 20 minutes.

2. Finish and Serve

Stir in the mango and cilantro and serve immediately.

Artichoke And Chickpea Loaf

Prep: 15 Minutes • Cook Time: 1 Hour 15 Minutes • Total: 15 Minutes • Serves: 6 To 8 Servings

Ingredients

1 large russet potato, peeled and cut into ½-inch dice

1 (10-ounce) package frozen artichoke hearts

¼ cup extra-virgin olive oil

1 large yellow onion, chopped

1½ cups or 1 (15.5-ounce) can chickpeas, drained and rinsed

¼ cup vegetable broth

2 tablespoons tahini

1½ tablespoons soy sauce

1½ tablespoons fresh lemon juice

2/3 cup wheat gluten flour (vital wheat gluten)

2⁄3 cup chickpea flour

½ cup nutritional yeast

1 teaspoon dried marjoram

1 teaspoon dried thyme

1 teaspoon salt

¼ teaspoon freshly ground black pepper

½ cup chopped oil-packed sun-dried tomatoes

¼ cup minced fresh parsley

Directions

1. **Preparing the Ingredients**

Preheat the oven to 375°F. Lightly oil a 9-inch loaf pan or square baking pan. Steam the potato and artichoke hearts (if using frozen) until tender. Blot off any excess moisture and set aside, reserving 2 of the artichoke hearts. Chop the reserved artichoke hearts and set aside.

In a large skillet, heat the oil over medium heat. Add the onion, cover, and cook until tender. Stir in the steamed potatoes and artichoke hearts.

Spoon the potato and artichoke mixture into a food processor. Add the chickpeas, broth, tahini, soy sauce, and lemon juice, then blend until smooth.

In a large bowl, combine both kinds of flour, the nutritional yeast, marjoram, thyme, salt and pepper, then stir to combine.

2. **Finish and Serve**

Add the wet ingredients to the dry ingredients. Add the sun-dried tomatoes, parsley, and reserved chopped artichoke hearts, and mix until well combined. Scrape the mixture into the prepared. Bake until firm and golden brown for about 1 hour. Let sit at room temperature for 15 minutes before slicing.

Lemon Broccoli Rabe

Prep: 10 Minutes • Cook Time: 10 Minutes • Total: 20 Minutes • Serves: 4

Ingredients

8 cups water

sea salt

2 bunches broccoli rabe, chopped

3 tablespoons extra-virgin olive oil

3 garlic cloves, minced

pinch of cayenne pepper

zest of 1 lemon

freshly ground black pepper

Directions

Preparing the Ingredients.

1. In a large pot, bring 8 cups of the water to a boil. Add a pinch of salt and the broccoli rabe. Cook until the broccoli rabe is slightly softened, about 2 minutes. Drain.

In a large sauté pan, heat the olive oil over medium-high heat until it shimmers. Add the garlic and cook until it is fragrant for about 30 seconds.

2. Finish and Serve

Stir in the broccoli rabe, cayenne, and lemon zest.

Season with salt and black pepper. Serve immediately.

Buttered Carrot Noodles with Kale

Prep: 10 Minutes • Cook Time: 10 Minutes • Total: 20 Minutes • Serves: 4

Ingredients

¼ cup vegan butter

½ cup chopped onion

1 pound carrots, peeled and sliced with a potato peeler or spiralizer

1 bunch lacinato kale, stemmed and thinly sliced

¼ cup chopped fresh parsley

¼ teaspoon sea salt

½ teaspoon black pepper

Directions

1. Preparing the Ingredients

In a large skillet, melt the butter over medium heat. Add the onion and sauté for 3 minutes, or until soft. Add the carrots and sauté for 3 minutes more, tossing in the butter until the carrots begin to brown on the edges.

2. Finish and Serve

Add the kale and sauté for an additional 2 minutes, or until wilted.

Mix in the parsley, salt, and pepper.

Tempeh And Vegetable Stir-Fry

Prep: 5 Minutes • Cook Time: 45 Minutes • Total: 50 Minutes • Serves: 4 Servings

Ingredients

8 ounces tempeh

Salt and freshly ground black pepper

2 teaspoons cornstarch

3 cups small broccoli florets

2 tablespoons canola or grapeseed oil

3 tablespoons soy sauce

2 tablespoons water

1 tablespoon mirin

½ teaspoon crushed red pepper

2 teaspoons toasted sesame oil

1 medium red bell pepper, cut into ½-inch slices

8 ounces white mushrooms, lightly rinsed, patted dry, and cut into ½-inch slices

2 garlic cloves, minced

3 tablespoons minced green onions

1 teaspoon grated fresh ginger

Directions

1. Preparing the Ingredients

In a medium saucepan of simmering water, cook the tempeh for 30 minutes. Drain, pat dry, and set aside to cool. Cut the tempeh into ½-inch cubes and place in a shallow bowl. Season with salt and black pepper, sprinkle with the cornstarch, then toss to coat. Set aside.

Lightly steam the broccoli until almost tender. Run under cold water to stop the cooking process and retain the bright green color. Set aside.

In a large skillet or wok, heat 1 tablespoon of the canola oil over medium-high heat. Add the tempeh and stir-fry until golden brown. Remove from the skillet and set aside.

In a small bowl, combine the soy sauce, water, mirin, crushed red pepper, and sesame oil. Set aside.

Reheat the same skillet over medium-high heat. Add the remaining 1 tablespoon of canola oil. Add the bell pepper and mushrooms and stir-fry until softened. Add the garlic, green onions, and ginger and stir-fry 1 minute. Add the steamed broccoli and fried tempeh and stir-fry for 1 minute.

2.   Finish and Serve

Stir in the soy sauce mixture and stir-fry until the tempeh and vegetables are hot and well coated with the sauce. Serve immediately.

Maple-Bourbon Acorn Squash

Prep: 10 Minutes • Cook Time: 30 Minutes • Total: 40 Minutes • Serves: 4

Ingredients

1 acorn squash (1 to 2 pounds), seeded and cut into ½-inch slices

½ cup bourbon

⅓ cup maple syrup

¼ cup vegan butter

¼ teaspoon ground cinnamon

2 pinches sea salt

Directions

1. **Preparing the Ingredients.**

Preheat the oven to 425°F. Line a baking sheet with parchment paper. Spread the squash slices on the prepared baking sheet and bake for 20 minutes.

Meanwhile, in a small saucepot, combine the bourbon, maple syrup, and butter. Melt over low heat and stir until well combined.

2. **Finish and Serve**

Flip the squash, drizzle with the bourbon mixture, and sprinkle with the cinnamon and salt. Bake for 8-10 more minutes until the liquid has started to caramelize and the squash is fork-tender.

Summer Squash Skillet

Prep: 10 Minutes • Cook Time: 10 Minutes • Total: 20 Minutes • Serves: 4

Ingredients

2 tablespoons extra-virgin olive oil divided

1 red onion, sliced

3 garlic cloves, sliced

2 medium green zucchini, halved lengthwise and sliced into ¼-inch half moons

2 medium yellow summer squashes, halved lengthwise and sliced into ¼-inch half moons

1 teaspoon Italian seasoning

½ teaspoon sea salt, plus more if needed

¼ teaspoon black pepper, plus more if needed

Directions

1. **Preparing the Ingredients.**

Heat 1 tablespoon of olive oil in a large skillet over medium heat. Add the red onion and sauté for 5 minutes, or until soft and stringy.

Add the garlic and sauté for 1 additional minute, or until fragrant.

Add the remaining 1 tablespoon of olive oil, the zucchini and squashes, Italian seasoning, salt, and pepper. Mix until well combined. Continue cooking for 4 to 6 minutes, tossing the vegetables every couple of minutes to ensure even cooking.

2. **Finish and Serve**

The zucchini and yellow squash will start to brown slightly and be fork-tender when ready. Add more salt and pepper to taste.

Roasted Asparagus with Balsamic Reduction

Prep: 10 Minutes • Cook Time: 25 Minutes • Total: 35 Minutes • Serves: 4

Ingredients

1½ pounds asparagus, trimmed

2 tablespoons extra-virgin olive oil

½ teaspoon sea salt

¼ teaspoon freshly ground black pepper

⅓ cup balsamic vinegar

juice and zest of 1 meyer lemon

Directions

1. **Preparing the Ingredients.**

Preheat the oven to 375°F. On a large rimmed baking sheet, toss the asparagus with the olive oil, salt and pepper, then spread the asparagus out into a single layer. Roast for 20-25 minutes, stirring once, until tender and beginning to brown.

While the asparagus is roasting, put the vinegar in a small saucepan and bring to boil over medium-high heat. Turn down the heat to low and simmer until reduced to a thick syrup for about 8 minutes.

2. Finish and Serve

When the asparagus is roasted, remove the baking sheet from the oven. Add the lemon juice and zest, then toss to coat.

Transfer to a serving platter and drizzle the balsamic reduction over the top. Serve immediately

Spaghetti Squash Primavera

Prep: 10 Minutes • Cook Time: 40 Minutes • Total: 50 Minutes • Serves: 4

Ingredients

1 large spaghetti squash (roughly 4 pounds), halved and seeded

3 tablespoons extra-virgin olive oil, divided

1 onion, chopped

2 cups chopped broccoli florets

½ cup pitted and sliced green olives

1 cup halved cherry tomatoes

3 garlic cloves, minced

1½ teaspoons Italian seasoning

¾ teaspoon sea salt

½ teaspoon black pepper

Pine nuts, for garnish (optional)

Walnut Parmesan or store-bought vegan Parmesan, for garnish (optional)

Red pepper flakes, for garnish (optional)

Directions

1. Preparing the Ingredients.

Preheat the oven to 400°F.

Line a baking sheet with parchment paper.

Brush the rims and the insides of both squash halves with 1 tablespoon of olive oil. Place on the prepared baking sheet, cut-sides down.

2. Bake

Bake for 35-45 minutes, until a fork can easily pierce the flesh. Set aside until cool enough to handle for 10-15 minutes.

While the squash is cooling, heat 1 tablespoon of olive oil in a large skillet over medium heat.

Add the onion and broccoli and sauté for 3 minutes, or until the onion is soft. Add the olives and tomatoes and cook for an additional 3-5 minutes, or until the broccoli is fork-tender and the tomatoes have started to wilt. Add the garlic and cook for 1 additional minute, or until fragrant.

3. Finish and Serve

Remove from the heat. Use a fork to gently pull the squash flesh from the skin and separate the flesh into strands. The strands wrap around the squash horizontally, so rake your fork in the same direction as the strands to make the longest spaghetti squash noodles. Toss the noodles into the skillet with the vegetables. Add 1 tablespoon of olive oil, Italian seasoning, salt and pepper and mix well to combine. Divide among bowls and garnish with pine nuts, Parmesan, and red pepper flakes if desired.

Sweet and Spicy Brussels Sprout Hash

Prep: 10 Minutes • Cook Time: 15 Minutes • Total: 25 Minutes • Serves: 4

Ingredients

3 tablespoons extra-virgin olive oil

2 shallots, thinly sliced

1½ pounds brussels sprouts, trimmed and cut into thin slices

3 tablespoons apple cider vinegar

1 tablespoon pure maple syrup

½ teaspoon sriracha sauce (or to taste)

sea salt

freshly ground black pepper

Directions

1. Preparing the Ingredients

2. In a large sauté pan, heat the olive oil over medium-high heat until it shimmers.

3. Add the shallots and brussels sprouts and cook, stirring frequently until the vegetables soften and begin to turn golden brown, about. Stir in the vinegar, using a spoon to scrape any browned bits from the bottom of the pan.

4. Finish and Serve

5. Stir in the maple syrup and sriracha. Simmer, stirring frequently until the liquid reduces, 3-5 minutes. Season with salt and pepper, then serve immediately.

Mindful Mushroom Stroganoff

Prep: 10 Minutes • Cook Time: 15 Minutes • Total: 25 Minutes • Serves: 6

Ingredients

1 tablespoon extra-virgin olive oil

1 onion, chopped

2 (8-ounce) packages baby bella or white button mushrooms, stemmed and sliced

4 garlic cloves, minced

¼ cup low-sodium vegetable broth

1 teaspoon paprika

½ teaspoon sea salt

½ teaspoon black pepper

¼ cup Sour Cream or store-bought vegan sour cream

4 tablespoons chopped fresh parsley, divided

1 pound pasta of your choice, cooked

Directions

1. Preparing the Ingredients

Heat the oil in a large skillet over medium heat.

Add the onion and mushrooms and sauté for 5 to 8 minutes, until the mushrooms are soft and have reduced in size. Add the garlic and sauté for 1 additional minute, or until fragrant. Add the broth, paprika, salt, and pepper and cook for 5 more minutes, or until well incorporated and heated through.

2. Finish and Serve

Remove from the heat and stir in the sour cream and 2 tablespoons of parsley. Toss with the cooked pasta, divide into 6 portions, and sprinkle with the remaining 2 tablespoons of parsley.

Eggplant & Chickpea Curry with Couscous

Prep: 10 Minutes • Cook Time: 10 Minutes • Total: 20 Minutes • Serves: 3

Ingredients

1 tablespoon extra-virgin olive oil

1 onion, chopped

1 eggplant, diced

Salt

1-inch piece fresh ginger, peeled and minced (optional)

1 (15-ounce) can chickpeas, drained and rinsed

1 tomato, chopped, or 1 cup canned diced tomatoes

1½ cups couscous

2¼ cups boiling water

6 tablespoons Coconut Curry Sauce

Chopped fresh cilantro or parsley, for garnish (optional)

Directions

1. Preparing the Ingredients

Heat the olive oil in a large skillet over medium heat.

Add the onion, eggplant, and a pinch of salt, and sauté for about 5 minutes until the vegetables are softened. Add the ginger (if using), chickpeas, and tomato, then cook for about 5 minutes more until everything is heated through and the tomato is softened. Meanwhile, in a medium heat-proof bowl, combine the couscous and boiling water. Cover and set aside.

Stir the coconut curry sauce into the cooked vegetables. Fluff the couscous with a fork.

2. Finish and Serve

Divide it among three bowls or lunch containers. Top with the veggies and chopped herbs (if using). Store the cooked ingredients in airtight containers for 4-5 days in the refrigerator, or up to 1 month in the freezer.

Lemon Broccoli Rabe

Prep: 10 Minutes • Cook Time: 10 Minutes • Total: 20 Minutes • Serves: 4

Ingredients

8 cups water

sea salt

2 bunches broccoli rabe, chopped

3 tablespoons extra-virgin olive oil

3 garlic cloves, minced

pinch of cayenne pepper

zest of 1 lemon

freshly ground black pepper

Directions

1. **Preparing the Ingredients**

In a large pot, bring 8 cups of the water to boil.

Add a pinch of salt and the broccoli rabe. Cook until the broccoli rabe is slightly softened. Drain. In a large sauté pan, heat the olive oil over medium-high heat until it shimmers. Add the garlic and cook until it is fragrant.

2. **Finish and Serve**

Stir in the broccoli rabe, cayenne, and lemon zest. Season with salt and black pepper.

Serve immediately.

Eggplant Parmesan

Prep: 10 Minutes • Cook Time: 15 Minutes • Total: 25 Minutes • Serves: 1

Ingredients

¼ cup nondairy milk

¼ cup bread crumbs or panko

2 tablespoons nutritional yeast (optional)

¼ teaspoon salt

4 (¼-inch-thick) eggplant slices, peeled if desired

1 tablespoon extra-virgin olive oil, plus more as needed

4 tablespoons Simple Homemade Tomato Sauce

4 teaspoons Parm Sprinkle

Directions

1. **Preparing the Ingredients.**

Put the milk in a shallow bowl. In another shallow bowl, stir together the bread crumbs, nutritional yeast (if using) and salt.

Dip one eggplant slice in the milk, making sure both sides get moistened. Dip it into the bread crumbs, flipping to coat both sides. Transfer to a plate and repeat to coat the remaining slices. Heat the olive oil in a large skillet over medium heat and add the breaded eggplant slices, making sure there is oil under each. Cook for 5-7 minutes until browned.

2. **Finish and Serve**

Flip, adding more oil as needed. Top each slice with 1 tablespoon tomato sauce and 1 teaspoon parm sprinkle. Cook for 5-7 minutes.

Per Serving Calories: 460; Protein: 23g; Total fat: 31g; Saturated fat: 4g; Carbohydrates: 31g; Fiber: 13g

Red Peppers and Kale

Prep: 5 Minutes • Cook Time: 15 Minutes • Total: 20 Minutes • Serves: 4

Ingredients

2 bunches kale, stalks removed and cut into small pieces

3 tablespoons extra-virgin olive oil

½ onion, chopped

2 red bell peppers, cut into strips

3 garlic cloves, minced

¼ teaspoon red pepper flakes

sea salt

freshly ground black pepper

Directions

1. **Preparing the Ingredients.**

In steamer basket in a pan, steam the kale until it softens. Remove from heat and set aside. Meanwhile, in a sauté pan, heat the olive oil over medium-high heat until it shimmers.

Add the onion and bell peppers and cook until soft. Add the garlic and cook until it is fragrant.

2. **Finish and Serve**

Remove from the heat and stir in the kale and red pepper flakes. Season with salt and black pepper, then serve immediately

Cauliflower Alfredo Your Way

Prep: 5 Minutes • Cook Time: 15 Minutes • Total: 20 Minutes • Serves: 6

Ingredients

4 cups bite-size cauliflower florets

1½ cups unsweetened soy or almond milk

¼ cup soft or silken tofu

Juice of ½ lemon

2 tablespoons Dijon mustard

1½ teaspoons onion powder

1½ teaspoons sea salt

1 teaspoon garlic powder

¼ teaspoon black pepper, plus more for garnish (optional)

1 pound pasta of your choice, cooked

vegan Parmesan, for garnish (optional)

Chopped fresh parsley, for garnish (optional)

Directions

1. **Preparing the Ingredients.**

Steam the cauliflower for 10-12 minutes until fork-tender, then transfer to a blender.

Add the milk, tofu, lemon juice, mustard, onion powder, salt, garlic powder, and pepper, then blend for 1-2 minutes until creamy and smooth.

2. Finish and Serve

Toss the cooked pasta with the sauce and divide among 6 serving bowls. Garnish with Parmesan, parsley, and more pepper if desired.

Sweet Potato Quesadilla

Prep: 10 Minutes • Cook Time: 10 Minutes • Total: 20 Minutes • Serves: 1

Ingredients

1 to 2 teaspoons extra-virgin olive oil, plus more as needed

¼ onion, chopped

Salt

½ cooked sweet potato

½ cup canned black beans, drained and rinsed

½ to 1 teaspoon chili powder

1 teaspoon freshly squeezed lime juice

1 large flour or corn tortilla

¼ cup grated vegan cheese (optional)

Loaded Guacamole, for serving

Salsa, for serving

Sour Cream, for serving

Directions

1. Preparing the Ingredients.

Heat the olive oil in a large skillet over medium heat.

Add the onion and a pinch of salt, and sauté for about 5 minutes, until the onion is soft. Meanwhile, in a medium bowl, mash together the sweet potato, black beans, chili powder, lime juice, and a pinch of salt. Stir the onion into the sweet potato mixture, adding another drizzle of olive oil if your sweet potatoes look dry.

Spread the mixture onto half of the tortilla, and sprinkle with the cheese (if using). Fold the other side of the tortilla over to close. Return the skillet to medium heat and add another drizzle of olive oil. Gently transfer the filled tortilla to the pan and cook for about 2 minutes. Flip the tortilla, adding another drizzle of olive oil if needed, and cook for about 2 minutes more, until lightly browned.

2. Finish and Serve

Transfer to a plate, slice in thirds, and enjoy with scoops of guacamole, sour cream, and salsa.

Per Serving Calories: 526; Protein: 17g; Total fat: 11g; Saturated fat: 2g; Carbohydrates: 93g; Fiber: 15g

Steamed Broccoli with Walnut Pesto

Prep: 5 Minutes • Cook Time: 10 Minutes • Total: 15 Minutes • Serves: 4

Ingredients

1 pound broccoli florets

2 cups chopped fresh basil

¼ cup extra-virgin olive oil

4 garlic cloves

½ cup walnuts

pinch of cayenne pepper

Directions

1. Preparing the Ingredients.

Put the broccoli in a large pot and cover with water.

Bring to a simmer over medium-high heat and cook until the broccoli is tender.

Meanwhile, in a food processor, combine the basil, olive oil, garlic, walnuts, and cayenne, then blend for ten 1-second pulses, scraping down the bowl halfway through processing.

2. Finish and Serve

Drain the broccoli and return to the pan. Toss with the pesto. Serve immediately

SALADS

Apple and Ginger Slaw

Prep: 10 Minutes • Cook Time: 0 Minutes • Total: 10 Minutes • Serves: 4

Ingredients

2 tablespoons extra-virgin olive oil

juice of 1 lemon, or 2 tablespoons prepared lemon juice

1 teaspoon grated fresh ginger

pinch of sea salt

2 apples, peeled and julienned

4 cups shredded red cabbage

Directions

Preparing the Ingredients.

In a small bowl, whisk together the olive oil, lemon juice, ginger, and salt, then set aside.

In a large bowl, combine the apples and cabbage.

Toss with the vinaigrette and serve immediately. Store leftovers in an airtight container in the refrigerator for up to 3 days.

Sunshine Fiesta Salad

Prep: 15 Minutes • Cook Time: 0 Minutes • Total: 15 Minutes • Serves: 4

Ingredients

FOR THE VINAIGRETTE

Juice of 2 limes

1 tablespoon extra-virgin olive oil

1 tablespoon maple syrup or agave

¼ teaspoon sea salt

FOR THE SALAD

2 cups cooked quinoa

1 tablespoon *Taco Seasoning* or store-bought taco seasoning

2 heads romaine lettuce, roughly chopped

1 (15-ounce) can black beans, rinsed and drained

1 cup cherry tomatoes, halved

1 cup frozen (and thawed) or fresh corn kernels

1 avocado, peeled, pitted, and diced

4 scallions, thinly sliced

12 tortilla chips, crushed

Directions

1. **To make the vinaigrette** In a small bowl, whisk together all the vinaigrette ingredients.

2. **To make the salad** In a medium bowl, mix together the quinoa and taco seasoning. In a large bowl, toss the romaine with the vinaigrette. Divide among 4 bowls. Top each bowl with equal amounts quinoa, beans,

tomatoes, corn, avocado, scallions, and crushed tortillas chips.

French-Style Potato Salad

Prep: 5 Minutes • Cook Time: 30 Minutes • Total: 15 Minutes • Serves: 4 To 6 Servings

Ingredients

1½ pounds small white potatoes, unpeeled

2 tablespoons minced fresh parsley

1 tablespoon minced fresh chives

1 teaspoon minced fresh tarragon or ½teaspoon dried

⅓ cup extra-virgin olive oil

2 tablespoons white wine or tarragon vinegar

¼ teaspoon freshly ground black pepper

Directions

1. **Preparing the Ingredients**

In a large pot of boiling salted water, cook the potatoes until tender but still firm for about 30 minutes. Drain and cut into ¼-inch slices. Transfer to a large bowl and add the parsley, chives, and tarragon. Set aside.

In a small bowl, combine the oil, vinegar, pepper.

2. **Finish and Serve**

Pour the dressing onto the potato mixture and toss gently to combine.

Taste and adjust the seasonings if necessary. Chill for 1-2 hours before serving.

Roasted Carrot Salad

Prep: 10 Minutes • Cook Time: 30 Minutes • Total: 40 Minutes • Serves: 3

Ingredients

4 carrots, peeled and sliced

1 to 2 teaspoons extra-virgin olive oil or coconut oil

½ teaspoon ground cinnamon or pumpkin pie spice

Salt

1 (15-ounce) can cannellini beans or navy beans, drained and rinsed

3 cups chopped hearty greens, such as spinach, kale, chard, or collards

⅓ cup dried cranberries or pomegranate seeds

⅓ cup slivered almonds or Cinnamon-Lime Sunflower Seeds

¼ cup Raspberry Vinaigrette or Cilantro-Lime *Dressing*, or 2 tablespoons freshly squeezed orange or lemon juice whisked with 2 tablespoons olive oil and a pinch of salt

Directions

1. **Preparing the Ingredients**

Preheat the oven or toaster oven to 400°F.

In a medium bowl, toss the carrots with the olive oil and cinnamon and season with salt. Transfer to a small tray, and roast for 15 minutes until browned around the edges.

Toss the carrots, add the beans, and roast for 15 minutes more. Let it cool while you prep the salad.

2.   Finish and Serve

Divide the greens among three plates or containers, top with the cranberries and almonds, and add the roasted carrots and beans.

Drizzle with the dressing of your choice. Store leftovers in an airtight container in the refrigerator for up to 1 week.

Roasted Potato Salad with Chickpeas and Tomatoes

Prep: 5 Minutes • Cook Time: 20 Minutes • Total:25Minutes • Serves: 4 To 6 Servings

Ingredients

1½ pounds Yukon Gold potatoes, cut into ½-inch dice

1 medium shallot, halved lengthwise and cut into ¼-inch slices

¼ cup extra-virgin olive oil

Salt and freshly ground black pepper

3 tablespoons white wine vinegar

1½ cups cooked or 1 (15.5-ounce) can chickpeas, drained and rinsed

⅓ cup chopped drained oil-packed sun-dried tomatoes

¼ cup green olives, pitted and halved

¼ cup chopped fresh parsley

Directions

1.   Preparing the Ingredients

Preheat the oven to 425°F.

In a large bowl, combine the potatoes, shallot, and 1 tablespoon of the oil. Season with salt and pepper and toss to coat. Transfer the potatoes and shallot to a baking sheet and roast, turning once, until tender and golden brown for about 20 minutes. Transfer to a large bowl and set aside to cool.

In a small bowl, combine the remaining 3 tablespoons oil with the vinegar and pepper. Add the chickpeas, tomatoes, olives, and parsley to the cooked potatoes and shallots.

2.   Finish and Serve

Drizzle with the dressing and toss gently to combine. Taste and adjust the seasonings if necessary. Serve warm or at room temperature.

Spinach and Pomegranate Salad

Prep: 10 Minutes • Cook Time: 0 Minutes • Total: 10 Minutes • Serves: 4

Ingredients

10 ounces baby spinach

seeds from 1 pomegranate

1 cup fresh blackberries

¼ red onion, thinly sliced

½ cup chopped pecans

¼ cup balsamic vinegar

¾ cup extra-virgin olive oil

½ teaspoon sea salt

½ teaspoon freshly ground black pepper

Directions

1.   Preparing the Ingredients.

In a large bowl, combine the spinach, pomegranate seeds, blackberries, red onion, and pecans.

In a small bowl, whisk together the vinegar, olive oil, salt, and pepper.

2.   Finish and Serve

Toss with the salad and serve immediately.

Cobb Salad with Portobello Bacon

Prep: 15 Minutes • Cook Time: 0 Minutes • Total: 15 Minutes • Serves: 4

Ingredients

2 heads romaine lettuce, finely chopped

1 pint cherry tomatoes, halved

1 avocado, peeled, pitted, and diced

1 cup frozen (and thawed) or fresh corn kernels

1 large cucumber, peeled and diced

Portobello Bacon or store-bought vegan bacon

4 scallions, thinly sliced

Unhidden Valley Ranch Dressing or store-bought vegan ranch dressing

Directions

1.   Preparing the Ingredients

Scatter a layer of romaine in the bottom of each of 4 salad bowls. With the following ingredients, create lines that cross the top of the romaine in this order: tomatoes, avocado, corn, cucumber, and portobello bacon.

2.   Finish and Serve

Sprinkle with the scallions and drizzle with ranch dressing

German-Style Potato Salad

Prep: 15 Minutes • Cook Time: 0 Minutes • Total: 15 Minutes • Serves: 4 To 6 Servings

Ingredients

1½ pounds white potatoes, unpeeled

½ cup extra-virgin olive oil

4 slices tempeh bacon, homemade or store-bought

1 medium bunch green onions, chopped

1 tablespoon whole-wheat flour

2 tablespoons sugar

⅓ cup white wine vinegar

¼ cup water

½ teaspoon salt

¼ teaspoon freshly ground black pepper

Directions

1. **Preparing the Ingredients**

In a large pot of boiling salted water, cook the potatoes until tender for about 30 minutes. Drain well and set aside to cool.

In a large skillet, heat the oil over medium heat. Add the tempeh bacon and cook until browned on both sides. Remove from skillet and set aside to cool.

Cut the cooled potatoes into 1-inch chunks and place in a large bowl. Crumble or chop the cooked tempeh bacon and add to the potatoes.

Reheat the skillet over medium heat. Add the green onions and cook for 1 minute to soften. Stir in the flour, sugar, vinegar, water, salt and pepper, and bring to boil, stirring until smooth.

2. **Finish and Serve**

Pour the hot dressing onto the potatoes. Stir gently to combine and serve.

Sweet Pearl Couscous Salad with Pear & Cranberries

Prep: 5 Minutes • Cook Time: 10 Minutes • Total: 15 Minutes • Serves: 4

Ingredients

1 cup pearl couscous

1½ cups water

Salt

¼ cup extra-virgin olive oil

¼ cup freshly squeezed orange juice

1 tablespoon sugar, maple syrup, or *Simple Syrup*

1 pear, cored and diced

½ cucumber, diced

¼ cup dried cranberries or raisins

Directions

1. **Preparing the Ingredients.**

In a small pot, combine the couscous, water, and a pinch of salt. Bring to boil over high heat, turn the heat to low, and cover the pot. Simmer for about 10 minutes until the couscous is al dente.

Meanwhile, in a large bowl, whisk together the olive oil, orange juice, and sugar. Season with salt and whisk again to combine.

2. **Finish and Serve**

Add the pear, cucumber, cranberries, and cooked couscous. Toss to combine. Store leftovers in an airtight container in the refrigerator for up to 1 week.

Per Serving Calories: 365; Protein: 6g; Total fat: 14g; Saturated fat: 2g; Carbohydrates: 55g; Fiber: 4g

Pear and Arugula Salad

Prep: 10 Minutes • Cook Time: 8 Minutes • Total: 18 Minutes • Serves: 4

Ingredients

¼ cup chopped pecans

10 ounces arugula

2 pears, thinly sliced

1 tablespoon finely minced shallot

2 tablespoons champagne vinegar

2 tablespoons extra-virgin olive oil

¼ teaspoon sea salt

¼ teaspoon freshly ground black pepper

¼ teaspoon dijon mustard

Directions

1. Preparing the Ingredients

Preheat the oven to 350°F.

Spread the pecans in a single layer on a baking sheet. Toast in the preheated oven until fragrant. Remove from the oven and let it cool.

In a large bowl, toss the pecans, arugula, and pears.

In a small bowl, whisk together the shallot, vinegar, olive oil, salt, pepper, and mustard.

2. Finish and Serve

Toss with the salad and serve immediately.

Quinoa Salad With Black Beans And Tomatoes

Prep: 5 Minutes • Cook Time: 20 Minutes • Total: 25 Minutes • Serves: 4 Servings

Ingredients

3 cups water

1½ cups quinoa, well rinsed

Salt

1½ cups cooked or 1 (15.5-ounce) can black beans, drained and rinsed

4 ripe plum tomatoes, cut into ¼-inch dice

⅓ cup minced red onion

¼ cup chopped fresh parsley

¼ cup extra-virgin olive oil

2 tablespoons sherry vinegar

¼ teaspoon freshly ground black pepper

Directions

1. Preparing the Ingredients

In a large saucepan, bring the water to boil over high heat. Add the quinoa, salt the water, and return to a boil. Reduce heat to low, cover, and simmer until the water is absorbed, about 20 minutes.

Transfer the cooked quinoa to a large bowl. Add the black beans, tomatoes, onion, and parsley.

In a small bowl, combine the olive oil, vinegar, salt to taste, and pepper.

2.   Finish and Serve

Pour the dressing over the salad and toss well to combine. Cover and set aside for 20 minutes before serving.

Apple, Pecan, and Arugula Salad

Prep: 10 Minutes • Cook Time: 0 Minutes • Total: 10 Minutes • Serves: 4

Ingredients

Juice of 1 lemon

2 tablespoons extra-virgin olive oil

1 tablespoon maple syrup

2 pinches sea salt

1 (5-ounce) package arugula

1 cup frozen (and thawed) or fresh corn kernels

½ red onion, thinly sliced

2 apples (preferably Gala or Fuji), cored and sliced

½ cup chopped pecans

¼ cup dried cranberries

Directions

1.   Preparing the Ingredients.

In a small bowl, whisk together the lemon juice, oil, maple syrup, and salt. In a large bowl, combine the arugula, corn, red onion, and apples. Add the lemon-juice mixture and toss to combine.

2.   Finish and Serve

Divide evenly among 4 plates and top with the pecans and cranberries.

Mediterranean Quinoa Salad

Prep: 5 Minutes • Cook Time: 20 Minutes • Total: 25 Minutes • Serves: 4 Servings

Ingredients

2 cups water

1 cup quinoa, well rinsed

Salt

1½cups cooked or 1 (15.5-ounce) can chickpeas, drained and rinsed

1 cup ripe grape or cherry tomatoes, halved

2 green onions, minced

½ medium English cucumber, peeled and chopped

¼ cup pitted brine-cured black olives

2 tablespoons toasted pine nuts

¼ cup small fresh basil leaves

1 medium shallot, chopped

1 garlic clove, chopped

1 teaspoon Dijon mustard

2 tablespoons white wine vinegar

¼ cup extra-virgin olive oil

Freshly ground black pepper

Directions

1. Preparing the Ingredients

In a large saucepan, bring the water to boil over high heat. Add the quinoa, salt the water, and return to boil. Reduce heat to low, cover, and simmer until water is absorbed.

Transfer the cooked quinoa to a large bowl. Add the chickpeas, tomatoes, green onions, cucumber, olives, pine nuts, and basil. Set aside.

2. Finish and Serve

In a blender or food processor, combine the shallot, garlic, mustard, vinegar, oil, then add salt and pepper. Process until well blended. Pour the dressing over the salad, toss gently to combine, and serve.

Apple, Pecan, and Arugula Salad

Prep: 10 Minutes • Cook Time: 0 Minutes • Total: 10 Minutes • Serves: 4

Ingredients

Juice of 1 lemon

2 tablespoons extra-virgin olive oil

1 tablespoon maple syrup

2 pinches sea salt

1 (5-ounce) package arugula

1 cup frozen (and thawed) or fresh corn kernels

½ red onion, thinly sliced

2 apples (preferably Gala or Fuji), cored and sliced

½ cup chopped pecans

¼ cup dried cranberries

Directions

1. Preparing the Ingredients.

In a small bowl, whisk together the lemon juice, oil, maple syrup, and salt. In a large bowl, combine the arugula, corn, red onion, and apples. Add the lemon-juice mixture and toss to combine.

2. Finish and Serve

Divide evenly among 4 plates and top with the pecans and cranberries.

Caesar Salad

Prep: 10 Minutes • Cook Time: 0 Minutes • Total: 10 Minutes • Serves: 1

Ingredients

FOR THE CAESAR SALAD

2 cups chopped romaine lettuce

2 tablespoons Caesar Dressing

1 serving Herbed Croutons or store-bought croutons

Vegan cheese, grated (optional)

MAKE IT A MEAL

½ cup cooked pasta

½ cup canned chickpeas, drained and rinsed

2 additional tablespoons Caesar Dressing

Directions

Preparing the Ingredients

In a large bowl, toss together the lettuce, dressing, croutons, and cheese (if using).

Add the pasta, chickpeas, and additional dressing. Toss to coat.

Classic Potato Salad

Prep: 10 Minutes • Cook Time: 15 Minutes • Total: 25 Minutes • Serves: 4

Ingredients

6 potatoes, scrubbed or peeled and chopped

Pinch salt

½ cup Creamy Tahini Dressing or vegan mayo

1 teaspoon dried dill (optional)

1 teaspoon Dijon mustard (optional)

4 celery stalks, chopped

2 scallions, white and light green parts only, chopped

Directions

1. **Preparing the Ingredients.**

2. Put the potatoes in a large pot, add the salt, and pour in enough water to cover. Bring the water to boil over high heat. Cook the potatoes for 15-20 minutes until soft. Drain and set aside to cool. (Alternatively, put the potatoes in a large microwave-safe dish with a bit of water. Cover and heat on high power for 10 minutes.)

3. **Finish and Serve**

4. In a large bowl, whisk together the dressing, dill (if using), and mustard (if using). Toss the celery and scallions with the dressing. Add the cooked, cooled potatoes and toss to combine. Store leftovers in an airtight container in the refrigerator for up to 1 week.

Per Serving Calories: 269; Protein: 6g; Total fat: 5g; Saturated fat: 1g; Carbohydrates: 51g; Fiber: 6g

Brown Rice and Pepper Salad

Prep: 15 Minutes • Cook Time: 0 Minutes • Total: 15 Minutes • Serves: 4

Ingredients

2 cups prepared brown rice

½ red onion, diced

1 red bell pepper, diced

1 orange bell pepper, diced

1 carrot, diced

¼ cup extra-virgin olive oil

2 tablespoons unseasoned rice vinegar

1 tablespoon soy sauce

1 garlic clove, minced

1 tablespoon grated fresh ginger

¼ teaspoon sea salt

¼ teaspoon freshly ground black pepper

Directions

1. **Preparing the Ingredients.**

In a large bowl, combine the rice, onion, bell peppers, and carrot. In a small bowl, whisk together the olive oil, rice vinegar, soy sauce, garlic, ginger, salt, and pepper.

2. Finish and Serve

Toss with the rice mixture and serve immediately.

Mediterranean Orzo & Chickpea Salad

Prep: 15 Minutes • Cook Time: 8 Minutes • Total: 23 Minutes • Serves: 4

Ingredients

¼ cup extra-virgin olive oil

2 tablespoons freshly squeezed lemon juice

Pinch salt

1½ cups canned chickpeas, drained and rinsed

2 cups orzo or other small pasta shape, cooked according to the package directions, drained, and rinsed with cold water to cool

2 cups raw spinach, finely chopped

1 cup chopped cucumber

¼ red onion, finely diced

Directions

1. Preparing the Ingredients.

In a large bowl, whisk together the olive oil, lemon juice, and salt. Add the chickpeas and cooked orzo, then toss to coat.

2. Finish and Serve

Stir in the spinach, cucumber, and red onion. Store leftovers in an airtight container in the refrigerator for up to 5 days.

Per Serving Calories: 233; Protein: 6g; Total fat: 15g; Saturated fat: 2g; Carbohydrates: 20g; Fiber: 5g

SNACKS AND SIDES

Chocolate-Cranberry Oatmeal Cookies

Prep: 5 Minutes • Cook Time: 15 Minutes • Total: 20 Minutes • Serves: About 2 Dozen Cookies

Ingredients

½ cup vegan margarine

1 cup sugar

¼ cup apple juice

1 cup whole-grain flour

1 teaspoon baking powder

½ teaspoon salt

1 teaspoon pure vanilla extract

1 cup old-fashioned oats

½ cup vegan semisweet chocolate chips

½ cup sweetened dried cranberries

Directions

1. **Preparing the Ingredients**

Preheat the oven to 375°F. In a large bowl, cream together the margarine and the sugar until light and fluffy. Blend in the juice.

Add the flour, baking powder, salt, and vanilla, blending well. Stir in the oats, chocolate chips, and cranberries, then mix well.

Drop the dough from a teaspoon onto an ungreased baking sheet.

3. **Bake**

Bake until nicely browned for about 15 minutes. Cool the cookies slightly before transferring to a wire rack to cool completely. Store in an airtight container.

Cashew-Chocolate Truffles

Prep: 15 Minutes • Cook Time: 0 Minutes • Plus 1 Hour To Set • Serves: 12 Truffles

Ingredients

1 cup raw cashews, soaked in water overnight

¾ cup pitted dates

2 tablespoons coconut oil

1 cup unsweetened shredded coconut, divided

1 to 2 tablespoons cocoa powder, to taste

Directions

1. **Preparing the Ingredients**.

In a food processor, combine the cashews, dates, coconut oil, ½ cup of shredded coconut, and cocoa powder. Pulse until fully incorporated; it will resemble chunky cookie dough. Spread the remaining ½ cup of shredded coconut on a plate.

Form the mixture into tablespoon-size balls and roll on the plate to cover with the shredded coconut. Transfer to a parchment paper–lined plate or baking sheet. Repeat to make 12 truffles.

2. Finish and Serve

Place the truffles in the refrigerator for 1 hour to set. Transfer the truffles to a storage container or freezer-safe bag and seal.

Per Serving (1 truffle): Calories 238: Fat: 18g; Protein: 3g; Carbohydrates: 16g; Fiber: 4g; Sugar: 9g; Sodium: 9mg

Banana Chocolate Cupcakes

Prep: 20 Minutes • Cook Time: 20 Minutes • Total: 40 Minutes • Serves: 12 Cupcakes

Ingredients

3 medium bananas

1 cup non-dairy milk

2 tablespoons almond butter

1 teaspoon apple cider vinegar

1 teaspoon pure vanilla extract

1¼ cups whole-wheat flour

½ cup rolled oats

¼ cup coconut sugar (optional)

1 teaspoon baking powder

½ teaspoon baking soda

½ cup unsweetened cocoa powder

¼ cup chia seeds, or sesame seeds

Pinch sea salt

¼ cup dark chocolate chips, dried cranberries, or raisins (optional)

Directions

1. Preparing the Ingredients

Preheat the oven to 350°F. Lightly grease the cups of two 6-cup muffin tins or line with paper muffin cups.

Put the bananas, milk, almond butter, vinegar, and vanilla in a blender and purée until smooth, or stir together in a large bowl until smooth and creamy.

Put the flour, oats, sugar (if using), baking powder, baking soda, cocoa powder, chia seeds, salt, and chocolate chips in another large bowl, then stir to combine. Mix together the wet and dry ingredients, stirring as little as possible.

2. Bake

Spoon into muffin cups and bake for 20-25 minutes. Take the cupcakes out of the oven and let them cool fully before taking out of the muffin tins since they'll be very moist.

Per Serving (1 cupcake) Calories: 215; Total fat: 6g; Carbs: 39g; Fiber: 9g; Protein: 6g

Minty Fruit Salad

Prep: 15 Minutes • Cook Time: 5 Minutes • Total: 20 Minutes • Serves: 4

Ingredients

¼ cup lemon juice (about 2 small lemons)

4teaspoons maple syrup or agave syrup

2 cups chopped pineapple

2 cups chopped strawberries

2 cups raspberries

1 cup blueberries

8 fresh mint leaves

Directions

1. Preparing the Ingredients

Beginning with 1 mason jar, add the ingredients in this order:

1 tablespoon of lemon juice, 1 teaspoon of maple syrup, ½ cup of pineapple, ½ cup of strawberries, ½ cup of raspberries, ¼ cup of blueberries, and 2 mint leaves.

2. Finish and Serve

Repeat to fill 3 more jars. Close the jars tightly with lids. Place the airtight jars in the refrigerator for up to 3 days.

Per Serving: Calories: 138; Fat: 1g; Protein: 2g; Carbohydrates: 34g; Fiber: 8g; Sugar: 22g; Sodium: 6mg

Sesame Cookies

Prep: 10 Minutes • Cook Time: 12 Minutes • Total: 22 Minutes • Serves: 3 Dozen Cookies

Ingredients

¾ cup vegan margarine, softened

½ cup light brown sugar

1 teaspoon pure vanilla extract

2 tablespoons pure maple syrup

¼ teaspoon salt

2 cups whole-grain flour

¾ cup sesame seeds, lightly toasted

Directions

1. Preparing the Ingredients

In a large bowl, cream together the margarine and sugar until light and fluffy. Blend in the vanilla, maple syrup, and salt. Stir in the flour and sesame seeds and mix well. Roll the dough into a cylinder about 2 inches in diameter. Wrap it in plastic wrap and refrigerate for 1 hour or longer. Preheat the oven to 325°F.

Slice the cookie dough into 1⁄8-inch-thick rounds and arrange on an ungreased baking sheet about 2 inches apart.

2. Bake

Bake until light brown for about 12 minutes. When completely cool, store in an airtight container.

Lime in the Coconut Chia Pudding

Prep: 10 Minutes • Chill Time: 20 Minutes • Total: 30 Minutes • Serves: 4

Ingredients

Zest and juice of 1 lime

1 (14-ounce) can coconut milk

1 to 2 dates, or 1 tablespoon coconut or other unrefined sugar, or 1 tablespoon maple syrup, or 10 to 15 drops pure liquid stevia

2 tablespoons chia seeds, whole or ground

2 teaspoons matcha green tea powder (optional)

Directions

1. Preparing the Ingredients.

Blend all the ingredients in a blender until smooth. Chill in the fridge for about 20 minutes, then serve topped with one or more of the topping ideas.

Try blueberries, blackberries, sliced strawberries, Coconut Whipped Cream, or toasted unsweetened coconut.

Per Serving Calories: 226; Total fat: 20g; Carbs: 13g; Fiber: 5g; Protein: 3g

Mango Coconut Cream Pie

Prep: 20 Minutes • Chill Time: 30 Minutes • Total: 50 Minutes • Serves: 8

Ingredients

FOR THE CRUST

½ cup rolled oats

1 cup cashews

1 cup soft pitted dates

FOR THE FILLING

1 cup canned coconut milk

½ cup water

2 large mangos, peeled and chopped, or about 2 cups frozen chunks

½ cup unsweetened shredded coconut

Directions

1. Preparing the Ingredients.

Put all the crust ingredients in a food processor and pulse until it holds together. If you don't have a food processor, chop everything as finely as possible and use ½ cup cashew or almond butter in place of half the cashews. Press the mixture down firmly into an 8-inch pie or springform pan.

Put the all filling ingredients in a blender and purée until smooth for about 1 minute. It should be very thick, so you may have to stop and stir until it's smooth.

Pour the filling into the crust, use a rubber spatula to smooth the top, and put the pie in the freezer until set. Once frozen, it should be set out for about 15 minutes to soften before serving.

2. Finish and Serve

Top with a batch of Coconut Whipped Cream scooped on top of the pie once it's set. Finish it off with a sprinkling of toasted shredded coconut.

Per Serving (1 slice) Calories: 427; Total fat: 28g; Carbs: 45g; Fiber: 6g; Protein: 8g

Cherry-Vanilla Rice Pudding (Pressure cooker)

Prep: 5 Minutes • Pressure: 30 Minutes • Total: 1 Hour, Minutes • Pressure Level: High • Release: Natural•

Serves 4-6

Ingredients

1 cup short-grain brown rice

1¾ cups nondairy milk, plus more as needed

1½ cups water

4 tablespoons unrefined sugar or pure maple syrup (use 2 tablespoons if you use a sweetened milk), plus more as needed

1 teaspoon vanilla extract (use ½ teaspoon if you use vanilla milk)

Pinch salt

¼ cup dried cherries *or* ½ cup fresh or frozen pitted cherries

Directions

1. Preparing the Ingredients

In your electric pressure cooker's cooking pot, combine the rice, milk, water, sugar, vanilla, and salt.

2. High pressure for 30 minutes

Close and lock the lid and ensure the pressure valve is sealed, then select High Pressure and set the time for 30 minutes.

3. Pressure Release

Once the cook time is complete, let the pressure release naturally, about 20 minutes. Once all the pressure has released, carefully unlock and remove the lid. Stir in the cherries and put the lid back on loosely for about 10 minutes. Serve, adding more milk or sugar, as desired.

PER SERVING Calories: 177; Total fat: 1g; Protein: 3g; Sodium: 27mg; Fiber: 2g

Chocolate Coconut Brownies

Prep: 5 Minutes • Cook Time: 35 Minutes • Total: 40 Minutes • Serves: 12 Brownies

Ingredients

1 cup whole-grain flour

½ cup unsweetened cocoa powder

1 teaspoon baking powder

½ teaspoon salt

1 cup light brown sugar

½ cup canola oil

¾ cup unsweetened coconut milk

1 teaspoon pure vanilla extract

1 teaspoon coconut extract

½ cup vegan semisweet chocolate chips

½ cup sweetened shredded coconut

Directions

1. Preparing the Ingredients

Preheat the oven to 350°F. Grease an 8-inch square baking pan and set aside. In a large bowl, combine the flour, cocoa, baking powder, and salt. Set aside.

In a medium bowl, mix together the sugar and oil until blended. Stir in the coconut milk and the extracts and blend until smooth.

Add the wet ingredients to the dry ingredients, then stir to blend. Fold in the chocolate chips and coconut.

2. Bake

Scrape the batter into the prepared baking pan and bake until the center is set and a toothpick inserted in the center comes out clean for 35-40 minutes.

3. Finish and Serve

Let the brownies cool for 30 minutes before serving. Store in an airtight container.

Strawberry Parfaits With Cashew Crème

Prep: 10 Minutes • Chill Time: 50 Minutes • • Serves: 4 Servings

Ingredients

½ cup unsalted raw cashews

4 tablespoons light brown sugar

½ cup plain or vanilla soy milk

¾ cup firm silken tofu, drained

1 teaspoon pure vanilla extract

2 cups sliced strawberries

1 teaspoon fresh lemon juice

Fresh mint leaves, for garnish

Directions

1. Preparing the Ingredients

In a blender, grind the cashews and 3 tablespoons of the sugar to a fine powder. Add the soy milk and blend until smooth. Add the tofu and vanilla, then continue to blend until smooth and creamy. Scrape the cashew mixture into a medium bowl, cover, and refrigerate for 30 minutes.

In a large bowl, combine the strawberries, lemon juice, and remaining 1 tablespoon sugar. Stir gently to combine and set aside at room temperature for 20 minutes.

2. Finish and Serve

Spoon alternating layers of the strawberries and cashew crème into parfait glasses or wineglasses, ending with a dollop of the cashew crème. Garnish with mint leaves and serve.

Peach-Mango Crumble (Pressure cooker)

Prep: 10 Minutes • Pressure: 6 Minutes • Total: 21 Minutes • Pressure Level: High • Release: Quick• Serves 4-6

Ingredients

3 cups chopped fresh or frozen peaches

3 cups chopped fresh or frozen mangos

4 tablespoons unrefined sugar or pure maple syrup, divided

1 cup gluten-free rolled oats

½ cup shredded coconut, sweetened or unsweetened

2 tablespoons coconut oil or vegan margarine

Directions

1. **Preparing the Ingredients** In a 6to 7-inch round baking dish, toss together the peaches, mangos, and 2 tablespoons of sugar. In a food processor, combine the oats, coconut, coconut oil, and remaining 2 tablespoons of sugar. Pulse until combined. (If you use maple syrup, you'll need less coconut oil. Start with just the syrup and add oil if the mixture isn't sticking together.) Sprinkle the oat mixture over the fruit mixture.

Cover the dish with aluminum foil. Put a trivet in the bottom of your electric pressure cooker's cooking pot and pour in a cup or two of water. Using a foil sling or silicone helper handles, lower the pan onto the trivet.

2. **High pressure for 6 minutes.** Close and lock the lid and ensure the pressure valve is sealed, then select High Pressure and set the time for 6 minutes.

3. **Pressure Release.** Once the cook time is complete, quick release the pressure, being careful not to get your fingers or face near the steam release. Once all the pressure has released, carefully unlock and remove the lid. Let cool for a few minutes before carefully lifting out the dish with oven mitts or tongs. Scoop out portions to serve.

PER SERVING Calories: 321; Total fat: 18g; Protein: 4g; Sodium: 2mg; Fiber: 7g

Ginger-Spice Brownies

Prep: 5 Minutes • Cook Time: 35 Minutes • Total: 45 Minutes • Serves: 12 Brownies

Ingredients

1¾ cups whole-grain flour

1 teaspoon baking powder

1 teaspoon baking soda

½ teaspoon salt

1 tablespoon ground ginger

½ teaspoon ground cinnamon

½ teaspoon ground allspice

3 tablespoons unsweetened cocoa powder

½ cup vegan semisweet chocolate chips

½ cup chopped walnuts

¼ cup canola oil

½ cup dark molasses

½ cup water

⅓ cup light brown sugar

2 teaspoons grated fresh ginger

Directions

1. Preparing the Ingredients

Preheat the oven to 350°F. Grease an 8-inch square baking pan and set aside. In a large bowl, combine the flour, baking powder, baking soda, salt, ground ginger, cinnamon, allspice, and cocoa. Stir in the chocolate chips and walnuts and set aside.

In medium bowl, combine the oil, molasses, water, sugar, and fresh ginger, then mix well.

Pour the wet ingredients into the dry ingredients and mix well.

Scrape the dough into the prepared baking pan. The dough will be sticky, so wet your hands to press it evenly into the pan.

2. Bake

Bake until a toothpick inserted in the center comes out clean, for 30-35 minutes. Cool on a wire rack 30 minutes before cutting. Store in an airtight container.

Zesty Orange-Cranberry Energy Bites

Prep: 10 Minutes • Chill Time: 15 Minutes • Total: 25 Minutes • Serves: 12 Bites

Ingredients

2 tablespoons almond butter, or cashew or sunflower seed butter

2 tablespoons maple syrup, or brown rice syrup

¾ cup cooked quinoa

¼ cup sesame seeds, toasted

1 tablespoon chia seeds

½ teaspoon almond extract, or vanilla extract

Zest of 1 orange

1 tablespoon dried cranberries

¼ cup ground almonds

Directions

1. Preparing the Ingredients

In a medium bowl, mix together the nut or seed butter and syrup until smooth and creamy. Stir in the rest of the ingredients, and mix to make sure the consistency is holding together in a ball. Form the mix into 12 balls.

Place them on a baking sheet lined with parchment or waxed paper and put in the fridge to set for about 15 minutes.

2. Finish and Serve

If your balls aren't holding together, it's likely because of the moisture content of your cooked quinoa. Add more nut or seed butter mixed with syrup until it all sticks together.

Per Serving (1 bite) Calories: 109; Total fat: 7g; Carbs: 11g; Fiber: 3g; Protein: 3g

Chocolate And Walnut Farfalle

Prep: 10 Minutes • Cook Time: 0 Minutes • Total: 10 Minutes • Serves: 4 Servings

Ingredients

½ cup chopped toasted walnuts

¼ cup vegan semisweet chocolate pieces

8 ounces farfalle

3 tablespoons vegan margarine

¼ cup light brown sugar

Directions

1. Preparing the Ingredients

In a food processor or blender, grind the walnuts and chocolate pieces until crumbly. Do not overprocess. Set aside.

In a pot of boiling salted water, cook the farfalle while stirring occasionally until al dente. Drain well and return to the pot.

2. Finish and Serve

Add the margarine and sugar, then toss to combine and melt the margarine.

Transfer the noodle mixture to a serving.

Mint Chocolate Chip Sorbet

Prep: 5 Minutes • Cook Time: 0 Minutes • Total: 5 Minutes • Serves: 1

Ingredients

1 frozen banana

1 tablespoon almond butter, or peanut butter, or other nut or seed butter

2 tablespoons fresh mint, minced

¼ cup or less non-dairy milk (only if needed)

2 to 3 tablespoons non-dairy chocolate chips, or cocoa nibs

2 to 3 tablespoons goji berries (optional)

Directions

Preparing the Ingredients.

1. Put the banana, almond butter, and mint in a food processor or blender and purée until smooth.

2. Add the non-dairy milk if needed to keep blending (but only if needed, as this will make the texture less solid). Pulse the chocolate chips and goji berries (if using) into the mix so they're roughly chopped up.

Per Serving Calories: 212; Total fat: 10g; Carbs: 31g; Fiber: 4g; Protein: 3g

Almond-Date Energy Bites

Prep: 5 Minutes • Chill Time: 15 Minutes • Total: 20 Minutes • Serves: 24 Bites

Ingredients

1 cup dates, pitted

1 cup unsweetened shredded coconut

¼ cup chia seeds

¾ cup ground almonds

¼ cup cocoa nibs, or non-dairy chocolate chips

Directions

1. **Preparing the Ingredients.**

Purée everything in a food processor until crumbly and sticking together, pushing down the sides whenever necessary to keep it blending. If you don't have a food processor, you can mash soft Medjool dates. But if you're using harder baking dates, you'll have to soak them, then try to purée them in a blender.

2. **Finish and Serve**

Form the mix into 24 balls and place them on a baking sheet lined with parchment or waxed paper. Put in the fridge to set for about 15 minutes. Use the softest dates you can find. Medjool dates are the best for this purpose. The hard dates you see in the baking aisle of your supermarket are going to take a long time to blend up. If you use those, try soaking them in water for at least an hour before you start, and then start draining.

Per Serving (1 bite) Calories: 152; Total fat: 11g; Carbs: 13g; Fiber: 5g; Protein: 3g

Pumpkin Pie Cups (Pressure cooker)

Prep: 5 Minutes • Pressure: 6 Minutes • Total: 20 Minutes • Pressure Level: High • Release: Quick• Serves 4-6

Ingredients

1 cup canned pumpkin purée

1 cup nondairy milk

6 tablespoons unrefined sugar or pure maple syrup (less if using sweetened milk), plus more for sprinkling

¼ cup spelt flour or all-purpose flour

½ teaspoon pumpkin pie spice

Pinch salt

Directions

1. **Preparing the Ingredients.** In a medium bowl, stir together the pumpkin, milk, sugar, flour, pumpkin pie spice, and salt. Pour the mixture into 4 heat-proof ramekins. Sprinkle a bit more sugar on the top of each, if you like. Put a trivet in the bottom of your electric pressure cooker's cooking pot and pour in a cup or two of water. Place the ramekins onto the trivet, stacking them if needed (3 on the bottom, 1 on top).

2. **High pressure for 6 minutes.** Close and lock the lid and ensure the pressure valve is sealed, then select High Pressure and set the time for 6 minutes.

3. **Pressure Release.** Once the cook time is complete, quick release the pressure. Once all the pressure has released, carefully unlock and remove the lid. Let cool for a few minutes before carefully lifting out the ramekins with oven mitts or tongs. Let cool for at least 10 minutes before serving.

PER SERVING Calories: 129; Total fat: 1g; Protein: 3g; Sodium: 39mg; Fiber: 3g

Coconut and Almond Truffles

Prep: 15 Minutes • Cook Time: 0 Minutes • Total: 15 Minutes • Serves: 8 Truffles

Ingredients

1 cup pitted dates

1 cup almonds

½ cup sweetened cocoa powder, plus extra for coating

½ cup unsweetened shredded coconut

¼ cup pure maple syrup

1 teaspoon vanilla extract

1 teaspoon almond extract

¼ teaspoon sea salt

Directions

1. **Preparing the Ingredients.**

In the bowl of a food processor, combine all the ingredients and process until smooth. Chill the mixture for about 1 hour.

2. **Finish and Serve**

Roll the mixture into balls and then roll the balls in cocoa powder to coat. Serve immediately or keep chilled until ready to serve.

Pecan And Date-Stuffed Roasted Pears

Prep: 10 Minutes • Cook Time: 30 Minutes • Total: 40 Minutes • Serves: 4 Servings

Ingredients

4 firm ripe pears, cored

1 tablespoon fresh lemon juice

½ cup finely chopped pecans

4 dates, pitted and chopped

1 tablespoon vegan margarine

1 tablespoon pure maple syrup

¼ teaspoon ground cinnamon

⅛ teaspoon ground ginger

½cup pear, white grape, or apple juice

Directions

1. **Preparing the Ingredients.**

Preheat the oven to 350°F. Grease a shallow baking dish and set aside. Halve the pears lengthwise and use a melon baller to scoop out the cores. Rub the exposed part of the pears with the lemon juice to avoid discoloration.

In a medium bowl, combine the pecans, dates, margarine, maple syrup, cinnamon, and ginger and mix well.

Stuff the mixture into the centers of the pear halves and arrange them in the prepared baking pan. Pour the juice over the pears.

2. **Bake**

Bake until tender, 30 to 40 minutes. Serve warm.

Lime-Macerated Mangos

Prep: 10 Minutes • Cooling Time: 6 Hours • • Serves: 4 To 6 Servings

Ingredients

3 ripe mangos

⅓ cup light brown sugar

2 tablespoons fresh lime juice

½ cup dry white wine

Fresh mint sprigs

Directions

1. **Preparing the Ingredients.**

Peel, pit, and cut the mangos into ½-inch dice. Layer the diced mango in a large bowl, sprinkling each layer with about 1 tablespoon of sugar. Cover with plastic wrap and refrigerate for 2 hours.

Pour in the lime juice and wine, mixing gently to combine with the mango. Cover and refrigerate for 4 hours.

About 30 minutes before serving time, bring the fruit to room temperature. To serve, spoon the mango and the liquid into serving glasses, then garnish with mint.

Fudgy Brownies (Pressure cooker)

Prep: 10 Minutes • Pressure: 5 Minutes • Total: 20 Minutes • Pressure Level: High • Release: Quick• Serves 4-6

Ingredients

3 ounces dairy-free dark chocolate

1 tablespoon coconut oil or vegan margarine

½ cup applesauce

2 tablespoons unrefined sugar

⅓ cup all-purpose flour

½ teaspoon baking powder

Pinch salt

Directions

1. **Preparing the Ingredients.** Put a trivet in your electric pressure cooker's cooking pot and pour in a cup or two of two of water. Select Sauté or Simmer. In a large heat-proof glass or ceramic bowl, combine the chocolate and coconut oil. Place the bowl over the top of your pressure cooker, as you would a double boiler. Stir

occasionally until the chocolate is melted, then turn off the pressure cooker. Stir the applesauce and sugar into the chocolate mixture. Add the flour, baking powder, and salt and stir just until combined. Pour the batter into 3 heat-proof ramekins. Put them in a heat-proof dish and cover with aluminum foil. Using a foil sling or silicone helper handles, lower the dish onto the trivet. (Alternately, cover each ramekin with foil and place them directly on the trivet, without the dish.)

2. **High pressure for 6 minutes.** Close and lock the lid and ensure the pressure valve is sealed, then select High Pressure and set the time for 5 minutes.

3. **Pressure Release.** Once the cook time is complete, quick release the pressure. Once all the pressure has released, carefully unlock and remove the lid.

Let cool for a few minutes before carefully lifting out the dish, or ramekins, with oven mitts or tongs. Let cool for a few minutes more before serving.

Top with fresh raspberries and an extra drizzle of melted chocolate.

PER SERVING Calories: 316; Total fat: 14g; Protein: 5g; Sodium: 68mg; Fiber: 5g

Chocolate-Banana Fudge

Prep: 10 Minutes • Chill Time: 2 Hours • • Serves: About 36 Pieces

Ingredients

1 ripe banana

¾ cup vegan semisweet chocolate chips

4 cups confectioners' sugar

1 teaspoon pure vanilla extract

Directions

1. **Preparing the Ingredients**

Line an 8-inch square baking pan with enough waxed paper or aluminum foil so that the ends hang over the edge of the pan. (This will help you get the fudge out of the pan later.) Set aside. Place the banana in a food processor and blend until smooth. Melt the chocolate chips in a double boiler or microwave, then add to the puréed banana along with the sugar and vanilla. Process until smooth.

Scrape the mixture into the prepared pan. Smooth the top and refrigerate until firm for at least 2 hours.

2. **Finish and Serve**

Once chilled, grip the waxed paper, lift the fudge from the pan, and transfer it to a cutting board. Remove and discard the waxed paper. Cut the fudge into small pieces and serve. Cover and refrigerate any leftovers.

Chocolate–Almond Butter Truffles

Prep: 15 Minutes • Chill Time: 45 Minutes • • Serves: About 24 Truffles

Ingredients

1 cup vegan semisweet chocolate chips

½ cup almond butter

2 tablespoons plain or vanilla soy milk

1 tablespoon pure vanilla extract

1 cup confectioners' sugar

2 tablespoons unsweetened cocoa powder

½ cup finely chopped toasted almonds

Directions

1. **Preparing the Ingredients**

Melt the chocolate in a double boiler or microwave.

In a food processor, combine the almond butter, soy milk, and vanilla and blend until smooth. Add the sugar, cocoa, and the melted chocolate and blend until smooth and creamy.

Transfer the mixture to a bowl and refrigerate until chilled for at least 45 minutes.

Roll the chilled mixture into 1-inch balls and place them on an ungreased baking sheet.

2. **Finish and Serve**

Place the ground almonds in a shallow bowl and roll the balls in them, turning to coat. Place the truffles on a serving platter, refrigerate for 30 minutes.

Chocolate Macaroons

Prep: 10 Minutes • Cook Time: 15 Minutes • Total: 25 Minutes • Serves: 8 Macaroons

Ingredients

1 cup unsweetened shredded coconut

2 tablespoons cocoa powder

⅔ cup coconut milk

¼ cup agave

pinch of sea salt

Directions

1. **Preparing the Ingredients.**

Preheat the oven to 350°F. Line a baking sheet with parchment paper. In a medium saucepan, cook all the ingredients over medium-high heat until a firm dough is formed. Scoop the dough into balls and place on the baking sheet.

2. **Bake**

Bake for 15 minutes, remove from the oven, and let it cool on the baking sheet. Serve cooled macaroons.

Chocolate Pudding

Prep: 5 Minutes • Cook Time: 0 Minutes • Total: 5 Minutes • Serves: 1

Ingredients

1 banana

2 to 4 tablespoons nondairy milk

2 tablespoons unsweetened cocoa powder

2 tablespoons sugar (optional)

½ ripe avocado or 1 cup silken tofu (optional)

Directions

Preparing the Ingredients.

In a small blender, combine the banana, milk, cocoa powder, sugar (if using), and avocado. (if using.) Purée until smooth. Alternatively, in a small bowl, mash the banana very well, then stir in the remaining ingredients.

.

Per Serving Calories: 244; Protein: 4g; Total fat: 3g; Saturated fat: 1g; Carbohydrates: 59g; Fiber: 8g

Lime and Watermelon Granita

Prep: 15 Minutes • Chilling Time: 6 Hours • • Serves: 4

Ingredients

8 cups seedless -watermelon chunks

juice of 2 limes, or 2 tablespoons prepared lime juice

½ cup sugar

strips of lime zest, for garnish

Directions

1. **Preparing the Ingredients**

In a blender or food processor, combine the watermelon, lime juice, and sugar and process until smooth. You may have to do this in two batches. After processing, stir well to combine both batches.

Pour the mixture into a 9-by-13-inch glass dish. Freeze for 2-3 hours. Remove from the freezer and use a fork to scrape the top layer of ice. Leave the shaved ice on top and return to the freezer.

2. **Finish and Serve**

In another hour, remove from the freezer and repeat. Do this a few more times until all the ice is scraped up. Serve frozen, garnished with strips of lime zest.

Chocolate-Covered Peanut Butter– Granola Balls

Prep: 15 Minutes • Chill Time: 30 Minutes •• Serves: About 3 Dozen Pieces

Ingredients

½ cup granola, homemade or store-bought

¼ cup light brown sugar

½ cup golden raisins

½ cup unsalted shelled sunflower seeds

¼ cup sesame seeds

1½ cups creamy peanut butter

2 cups vegan semisweet chocolate chips

Directions

1. **Preparing the Ingredients**

In a food processor, pulse together the granola, sugar, raisins, sunflower seeds, and sesame seeds. Blend in the peanut butter a little at a time to form a smooth dough. Refrigerate until chilled, for several hours or overnight. Form the mixture into 1-inch balls and set aside. Melt the chocolate in a double boiler or microwave.

2. **Finish and Serve**

Dip the balls into the melted chocolate and arrange on an ungreased baking sheet. Refrigerate until firm, about 30 minutes, and serve.

Spiced Apple Chia Pudding

Prep: 5 Minutes • Chill Time: 30 Minutes • Total: 35 Minutes • Serves: 1

Ingredients

½ cup unsweetened applesauce

¼ cup nondairy milk or canned coconut milk

1 tablespoon chia seeds

1½ teaspoons sugar

Pinch ground cinnamon or pumpkin pie spice

Directions

Preparing the Ingredients.

In a small bowl, stir together the applesauce, milk, chia seeds, sugar, and cinnamon. Enjoy as is, or let sit for 30 minutes so the chia seeds soften and expand.

Per Serving Calories: 153; Protein: 3g; Total fat: 5g; Saturated fat: 1g; Carbohydrates: 26g; Fiber: 10g

Coconut-Banana Pudding

Prep: 4 Minutes • Cook Time: 5 Minutes • Overnight To Set • Serves: 4

Ingredients

3 bananas, divided

1 (13.5-ounce) can full-fat coconut milk

¼ cup organic cane sugar

1 tablespoon cornstarch

1 teaspoon vanilla extract

2 pinches sea salt

6 drops natural yellow food coloring (optional)

Ground cinnamon, for garnish

Directions

1. **Preparing the Ingredients.**

Combine 1 banana, the coconut milk, sugar, cornstarch, vanilla, and salt in a blender. Blend until smooth and creamy. If you're using food coloring, add it to the blender now and blend until the color is evenly dispersed.

Transfer to a saucepot and bring to boil over medium-high heat. Immediately reduce to a simmer and whisk for 3 minutes, or until the mixture thickens to a thin pudding and sticks to a spoon.

Transfer the mixture to a container and allow to cool for 1 hour. Cover and refrigerate overnight to set.

2. Finish and Serve

When you're ready to serve, slice the remaining 2 bananas and build individual servings as follows: pudding, banana slices, pudding, and so on until a single-serving dish is filled to the desired level. Sprinkle with ground cinnamon

Caramelized Pears with Balsamic Glaze

Prep: 5 Minutes • Cook Time: 15 Minutes • Total: 20 Minutes • Serves: 4

Ingredients

1 cup balsamic vinegar

¼ cup plus 3 tablespoons brown sugar

¼ teaspoon grated nutmeg

pinch of sea salt

¼ cup coconut oil

4 pears, cored and cut into slices

Directions

1. Preparing the Ingredients.

In a medium saucepan, heat the balsamic vinegar, ¼ cup of the brown sugar, the nutmeg, and salt over medium-high heat, stirring to thoroughly incorporate the sugar. Allow to simmer while stirring occasionally until the glaze reduces by half.

Meanwhile, heat the coconut oil in a large sauté pan over medium-high heat until it shimmers. Add the pears to the pan in a single layer. Cook until they turn golden.

2. Finish and Serve

Add the remaining 3 tablespoons brown sugar and continue to cook and stir occasionally until the pears caramelize.

Place the pears on a plate. Drizzle with balsamic glaze and serve.

Spicy Chocolate Cake With Dark Chocolate Glaze

Prep: 15 Minutes • Cook Time:30 Minutes • Total: 45 Minutes • Serves: 8 Servings

Ingredients

Cake

1¾ cups whole-grain flour

1 cup light brown sugar

¼cup unsweetened cocoa powder

1 teaspoon baking soda

½ teaspoon baking powder

1½ teaspoons ground cinnamon

¼ teaspoon ground cayenne

⅓ cup extra olive oil

1 tablespoon apple cider vinegar

1½ teaspoons pure vanilla extract

1 cup cold water

Glaze

2 (1-ounce) squares unsweetened vegan chocolate

¼ cup plain or vanilla soy milk

½ cup light brown sugar

2 tablespoons vegan margarine

½ teaspoon pure vanilla extract

Pinch ground cayenne

Directions

1. **Preparing the Ingredients**

Make the cake: Preheat the oven to 350°F. Grease a 9-inch round cake pan and set aside.

In a large bowl, combine the flour, sugar, cocoa, baking soda, baking powder, cinnamon, and cayenne.

In a medium bowl, combine the oil, vinegar, vanilla, and water. Stir the wet ingredients into the dry ingredients, mixing until combined.

2. **Bake**

Pour the batter into the prepared pan and bake until a toothpick inserted into the center comes out clean. Cool the cake in the pan for 10-15 minutes, then invert it onto a wire rack and let the cake cool completely while you make the glaze.

3. **Finish and Serve**

In a double boiler, combine the chocolate and soy milk and cook and stir constantly until the chocolate is melted. Stir in the sugar and cook while stirring constantly. Remove from heat and stir in the margarine, vanilla, and cayenne. Drizzle the glaze over the cooled cake. Refrigerate the cake to let the glaze set before serving.

Blueberry-Peach Crisp

Prep: 15 Minutes • Cook Time: 30 Minutes • Total: 45 Minutes • Serves: 8 Servings

Ingredients

4 fresh ripe peaches, peeled, pitted, and cut into ¼-inch slices

2 cups fresh blueberries

1 tablespoon cornstarch

¾ cup light brown sugar

2 teaspoons fresh lemon juice

1 teaspoon ground cinnamon

½ cup whole-grain flour

½ cup old-fashioned oats

3 tablespoons vegan margarine

Directions

1. **Preparing the Ingredients**

Preheat the oven to 375°F. Lightly oil a 9-inch square baking pan and set aside. In a large bowl, combine the peaches, blueberries, cornstarch, ¼cup of the sugar, lemon juice, and ½teaspoon of the cinnamon. Mix gently and spoon into the prepared baking pan. Set aside.

In small bowl, combine the flour, oats, margarine, the remaining ½cup sugar, and the remaining ½teaspoon cinnamon. Use a pastry blender or fork to mix until crumbly.

2. **Bake**

Sprinkle the topping over the fruit mixture and bake until the top is browned and bubbly in the center, 30 to 40 minutes. Serve warm.

Salted Coconut-Almond Fudge

Prep: 5 Minutes • Set Time: 1 Hour • • Serves: 12

Ingredients

¾ cup creamy almond butter

½ cup maple syrup

⅓ cup coconut oil, softened or melted

6 tablespoons fair-trade unsweetened cocoa powder

1 teaspoon coarse or flaked sea salt

Directions

1. **Preparing the Ingredients.**

Line a loaf pan with a double layer of plastic wrap. Place one layer horizontally in the pan with a generous amount of overhang, and the second layer vertically with a generous amount of overhang.

In a medium bowl, gently mix together the almond butter, maple syrup, and coconut oil until well combined and smooth. Add the cocoa powder and gently stir it into the mixture until well combined and creamy.

Pour the mixture into the prepared pan and sprinkle with sea salt. Bring the overflowing edges of the plastic wrap over the top of the fudge to completely cover it. Place the pan in the freezer for at least 1 hour or overnight, or until the fudge is firm.

2. **Finish and Serve**

Remove the pan from the freezer and lift the fudge out of the pan using the plastic-wrap overhangs to pull it out. Transfer to a cutting board and cut into 1-inch pieces.

Quick Apple Crisp

Prep: 10 Minutes • Cook Time: 45 Minutes • Total: 55 Minutes • Serves: 6 Servings

Ingredients

5 Granny Smith apples, peeled, cored, and cut into ¼-inch slices

½ cup pure maple syrup

1 tablespoon fresh lemon juice

1 teaspoon ground cinnamon

½ cup whole-grain flour

½ cup old-fashioned oats

½ cup finely chopped walnuts or pecans

2⁄3 cup light brown sugar

½ cup vegan margarine, softened

Directions

1. Preparing the Ingredients

Preheat the oven to 350°F. Lightly oil a 9-inch square baking pan. Place the apples in the prepared pan. Drizzle the maple syrup and lemon juice over the apples and sprinkle with ½teaspoon of the cinnamon. Set aside.

In a medium bowl, mix the flour, oats, walnuts, sugar, and the remaining ½teaspoon cinnamon. Use a pastry blender to cut in the margarine until the mixture resembles coarse crumbs.

2. Bake

Spread the topping over the apples and bake until bubbly and lightly browned on top, about 45 minutes. Serve warm.

Mixed Berries and Cream

Prep: 10 Minutes • Cook Time: 0 Minutes • Total: 10 Minutes • Serves: 4

Ingredients

two 15-ounce cans full-fat coconut milk

3 tablespoons agave

½ teaspoon vanilla extract

1 pint fresh blueberries

1 pint fresh raspberries

1 pint fresh strawberries, sliced

Directions

1. Preparing the Ingredients.

Refrigerate the coconut milk overnight. When you open the can, the liquid will have separated from the solids. Spoon out the solids and reserve the liquid for another purpose.

In a medium bowl, whisk the agave and vanilla extract into the coconut solids.

2. Finish and Serve

Divide the berries among four bowls.

Top with the coconut cream.

Serve immediately.

Peanut Butter Cups

Prep: 20 Minutes • Cook Time: 0 Minutes • Total: 20 Minutes • Serves: 12 Cups

Ingredients

1½ cups vegan chocolate chips, divided

½ cup peanut butter, almond or cashew butter, or sunflower seed butter

¼ cup packed brown sugar

2 tablespoons nondairy milk

Directions

1. **Preparing the Ingredients.**

Line the cups of a muffin tin with paper liners or reusable silicone cups.

In a small microwave-safe bowl, heat ¾ cup of the chocolate chips on high power for 1 minute. Stir. Continue heating in 30-second increments, stirring after each, until the chocolate is melted.

Pour about 1½ teaspoons of melted chocolate into each prepared muffin cup. Set aside, and allow them to harden.

In a small bowl, stir together the peanut butter, brown sugar, and milk until smooth. Scoop about 1½ teaspoons of the mixture on top of the chocolate base in each cup. It's okay if the chocolate is not yet hardened.

2. **Finish and Serve**

Melt the remaining ¾ cup of chocolate chips using the directions in step 1. Pour another 1½ teaspoons of chocolate on top of the peanut butter in each cup, softly spreading it to cover. Let the cups sit until the chocolate hardens, about 15 minutes in the refrigerator or several hours on the counter. Leftovers will keep in the refrigerator for up to 2 weeks.

Per Serving (1 cup) Calories: 227; Protein: 4g; Total fat: 14g; Saturated fat: 6g; Carbohydrates: 22g; Fiber: 3g

Caramelized Bananas

Prep: 5 Minutes • Cook Time: 10 Minutes • Total: 15 Minutes • Serves: 2

Ingredients

2 tablespoons vegan margarine or coconut oil

2 bananas, peeled, halved crosswise and then lengthwise

2 tablespoons dark brown sugar, demerara sugar, or coconut sugar

2 tablespoons spiced apple cider

Chopped walnuts, for topping

Directions

1. **Preparing the Ingredients.**

Melt the margarine in a nonstick skillet over medium heat. Add the bananas, then cook for 2 minutes. Flip, and cook for another 2 minutes.

Sprinkle the sugar and cider into the oil around the bananas and cook for 2-3 minutes until the sauce thickens and caramelizes around the bananas.

2. **Finish and Serve**

Carefully scoop the bananas into small bowls, then drizzle with any remaining liquid in the skillet. Sprinkle with walnuts.

Carrot Cake

Prep: 15 Minutes • Cook Time: 45 Minutes • Total: 60 Minutes • Serves: 8 Servings

Ingredients

2 cups whole-grain flour

2 teaspoons baking powder

1 teaspoon baking soda

2 teaspoons ground cinnamon

½ teaspoon ground allspice

1 teaspoon salt

1 cup light brown sugar

½ cup plain or vanilla soy milk

½ cup canola or other neutral oil

¼ cup pure maple syrup

2 teaspoons pure vanilla extract

2 cups finely shredded carrots

½ cup golden raisins

1 recipe "Cream Cheese" Frosting

Directions

1. Preparing the Ingredients

Preheat the oven to 350°F. Grease a 9-inch square baking pan and set aside.

In a medium bowl, mix the flour, baking powder, baking soda, cinnamon, allspice, and salt.

In a large bowl, combine the sugar, soy milk, oil, maple syrup, and vanilla, then add the wet ingredients to the dry ingredients. Stir in the carrots and raisins until mixed.

2. Bake

Scrape the batter into the prepared pan. Bake until a toothpick comes out clean.

Let the cake cool in the pan for 15 minutes, then invert onto a wire rack to cool completely. When cooled, frost the cake with "cream cheese" frosting.

Spice Cake With Mango And Lime

Prep: 15 Minutes • Cook Time: 45 Minutes • Total: 60 Minutes • Serves: 8 Servings

Ingredients

1½ cups whole-grain flour

¾ cup light brown sugar

¼ cup yellow cornmeal

1 teaspoon baking soda

½ teaspoon salt

½ teaspoon baking powder

½ teaspoon ground cinnamon

½ teaspoon ground allspice

½ teaspoon ground ginger

1 cup applesauce

⅓ cup canola or other neutral oil

2 teaspoons grated lime zest

2 tablespoons water

1 ripe mango, peeled, pitted, and chopped

Directions

1. Preparing the Ingredients

Preheat the oven to 350°F. Lightly oil a 9-inch round cake pan and set aside.

In a large bowl, combine the flour, sugar, cornmeal, baking soda, salt, baking powder, cinnamon, allspice, and ginger, then set aside.

In a medium bowl, combine the applesauce, oil, lime zest, and water while stirring to blend.

Fold in the mango. Add the wet ingredients to the dry ingredients and mix to combine.

2. Bake

Pour the batter into the prepared baking pan. Bake until a toothpick inserted in the center comes out clean. Let the cake cool in the pan for 10 minutes, then invert onto a wire rack to cool completely before slicing.

Dessert Crêpes

Prep: 5 Minutes • Cook Time: 10 Minutes • Total: 15 Minutes • Serves: 10 Crêpes

Ingredients

1 ⅓ cups plain or vanilla soy milk

1 cup whole-grain flour

⅓ cup firm tofu, drained and crumbled

3 tablespoons vegan margarine, melted

2 tablespoons light brown sugar

1½ teaspoons pure vanilla extract

½ teaspoon baking powder

⅛ teaspoon salt

Canola or other neutral oil, for cooking

Directions

1. Preparing the Ingredients

In a blender, combine all the ingredients (except the oil for cooking) and blend until smooth.

Heat a nonstick medium skillet or crêpe pan over medium-high heat. Coat the pan with a small amount of oil. Pour about 3 tablespoons of the batter into the center of the skillet and tilt the pan to spread the batter out thinly. Cook until golden on both sides, flipping once. Transfer to a platter and repeat with the remaining batter, oiling the pan as needed.

2. Finish and Serve

The crêpes can now be used in the recipes below or topped with your favorite dessert sauce or sautéed fruit. These taste best if used on the same day that they are made.

Strawberry Sorbet

Prep: 15 Minutes • Cook Time: 0 Minutes • Total: 15 Minutes • Serves: About 1 Pint

Ingredients

½cup light brown sugar

½cup water

2 cups hulled strawberries

2 teaspoons fresh lemon juice

Directions

1. Preparing the Ingredients

In a medium saucepan, combine the sugar and water. Cook and stir over low heat until sugar is dissolved. Increase the heat to high and bring to boil, then remove from heat. Transfer to a heatproof bowl and refrigerate until chilled for about 2 hours.

In a blender or food processor, combine the strawberries and lemon juice, then blend until smooth. Add the cooled sugar syrup to the strawberry mixture and process until smooth.

2. Finish and Serve

Freeze the mixture in an ice cream maker according to the manufacturer's directions. When the mixture is finished churning in the machine, it will be soft, but ready to eat. For a firmer sorbet, transfer to a freezer-safe container and freeze for no more than 1-2 hours for the best flavor and texture.

Prep: 15 Minutes • Cook Time: 20 Minutes • Total: 35 Minutes • Serves: About 2 Cups

Ingredients

1 cup water

1 cup dried mixed fruit

1 teaspoon fresh lemon juice

½ teaspoon ground cinnamon

¼ cup apple juice

Directions

1. Preparing the Ingredients

In a large saucepan, combine the water, dried fruit, lemon juice, and cinnamon. Cover and bring to boil over high heat. Reduce heat to medium and simmer for 20 minutes.

Remove from the heat and set aside to cool for 15 minutes, then transfer to a blender or food processor and process until smooth. Add the apple juice and process until blended.

2. Finish and Serve

Return the sauce to the saucepan and heat on low until warm. Store leftover sauce covered in the refrigerator for up to 3 days.

Winter Fruit Sauce

Chocolate-Coconut Bars

Prep: 20 Minutes • Chill Time: 20 Minutes • • Serves: 16 Bars

Ingredients

¼ cup coconut oil or unsalted vegan margarine, plus more for preparing the baking dish (optional)

2 cups unsweetened shredded coconut

¼ cup sugar

2 tablespoons maple syrup or Simple Syrup

1 cup vegan chocolate chips

Directions

1. **Preparing the Ingredients.**

Coat an 8-inch square baking dish with coconut oil or line it with parchment paper, set aside.

In a small bowl, stir together the coconut, sugar, maple syrup, and coconut oil. Transfer the mixture to the prepared baking dish, and press it down firmly with the back of a spoon.

In a small microwave-safe bowl, heat the chocolate chips on high power for 1 minute. Stir. Continue heating in 30-second increments, stirring after each, until the chocolate is melted.

2. **Finish and Serve**

Pour the melted chocolate over the coconut base, and let it sit until the chocolate hardens, about 20 minutes. Cut into 16 bars. They will keep, covered and refrigerated, for up to 1 week.

Per Serving (1 bar) Calories: 305; Protein: 3g; Total fat: 26g; Saturated fat: 22g; Carbohydrates: 19g; Fiber: 6g